Daredevil Research

Studies in the
Postmodern Theory of Education

Joe L. Kincheloe and Shirley R. Steinberg
General Editors

Vol. 21

PETER LANG
New York • Washington, D.C./Baltimore
Bern • Frankfurt am Main • Berlin • Vienna • Paris

DAREDEVIL RESEARCH

Re-creating Analytic Practice

EDITED BY

Janice A. Jipson &
Nicholas Paley

PETER LANG
New York • Washington, D.C./Baltimore
Bern • Frankfurt am Main • Berlin • Vienna • Paris

Library of Congress Cataloging-in-Publication Data

Daredevil research: re-creating analytic practice/
edited by Nicholas B. Paley, Janice A Jipson.
p. cm. — (Counterpoints; vol. 21)
Includes bibliographical references and index.
1. Education—Research—Philosophy. 2. Education—Research—
Methodology. 3. Deconstruction. I. Paley, Nicholas. II. Jipson, Janice.
III. Series: Counterpoints (New York, N.Y.); vol. 21.
LB1028.D32   370'.78—dc20   95-22935
ISBN 0-8204-2776-4
ISSN 1058-1634

Die Deutsche Bibliothek-CIP-Einheitsaufnahme

Daredevil research: re-creating analytic practice/ edited by Nicholas B. Paley;
Janice A. Jipson. (New York; Washington, D.C./Baltimore; Bern; Frankfurt
am Main; Berlin; Vienna; Paris: Lang.
(Counterpoints; Vol. 21)
ISBN 0-8204-2776-4
NE: GT

Cover design by James F. Brisson.

The paper in this book meets the guidelines for permanence and durability
of the Committee on Production Guidelines for Book Longevity
of the Council of Library Resources

Dedication

We dedicate this book
to our respective parents,
Nicholas Miroslav Paley
and Mary Temoshok Paley,
and John Adolph Jipson
and Jeanette Nelson Jipson,
who by their examples
and their lives
taught us to take risks.

Contents

Acknowledgments

Many people made this book possible. We would like to extend our appreciation to Michael Apple and Thomas Romberg at the University of Wisconsin who greatly influenced our initial thinking about research methodology and the representation of knowledge. We also would to thank our colleagues, Kathleen Casey, Maxine Freund, Linda Mauro, Gary Price, and Rob Proudfoot who, through their teaching and scholarship during the past decade, have supported us in the development of our ideas. Further, we would like to extend our thanks to our students who helped us formulate, clarify, and articulate the place of the imaginative and the experimental in educational practice.

This book was also made possible by the contributing authors: Karen Anijar, Chelsea Bailey, Thomas Barone, Donald Blumenfeld-Jones, Deb Casey, Joan Montgomery Halford, Gunilla Holm, Petra Munro, and Bruce Wilson. We thank all of them for believing in the value of these collaborations.

Finally, the patience, careful work, and inventiveness of Nona Reuter and Chris Myers at Peter Lang in facilitating production of this text has been absolutely essential. Thank you.

Contributors

Karen Anijar is an Assistant Professor of Education at California Polytechnic University at Pomona. She is currently working on two books: *The Social Curriculum of Star Trek in the Schools* and *The Political Economy of Nurture*

Chelsea Bailey is a doctoral student in Curriculum and Instruction at the University of Wisconsin-Madison. Her dissertation, *Disciplining Desire: Regulating Bodies in the Preschool Classroom*, will be completed this year.

Thomas Barone is Professor in the College of Education at Arizona State University. Since 1978 his writing has explored conceptually and through examples the possibilities of a variety of arts-based approaches to contextualizing and theorizing about fundamental educational issues.

Donald Blumenfeld-Jones is Assistant Professor in the College of Education at Arizona State University, specializing in philosophy and curriculum studies. He has also been a professional dancer since 1970. His most recent work focuses on the arts, educational research, and teaching.

Deb Casey coordinates services for non-traditional students at the University of Oregon; is the mother of two daughters, Josiephine and Anna; is completing the manuscripts, *Motherwork*, and *Gathering Up Sister Time;* and works to document/implement/develop options for on-site care and healthy family/work approaches.

Joan Montgomery Halford is a staff writer/analyst at the Association for Supervision and Curriculum Development. Her monographs address equity, diversity, and poverty issues in school and community.

Gunilla Holm is an Associate Professor of Education at Western Michigan University. She is the co-editor (with Paul Farber and Eugene Provenzo) of *Schooling in the Light of Popular Culture.* She has written on issues of cultural diversity in numerous educational journals. Her research interests focus on gender, social class and ethnicity in education and popular culture.

Janice Jipson is an Associate Professor of Education at Carroll College. Her recent books include *Repositioning Feminism and Education: Perspectives on Educating for Social Change* (with Petra Munro, Susan Victor, Karen Jones, and Gretchen Freed Rowland) and *Intersections: Feminisms/Early Childhoods* (with Mary Hauser) to be released in October 1996.

Petra Munro is an Assistant Professor of Education at Louisiana State University. In addition to her book (with Janice Jipson, et al.), *Repositioning Feminism and Education: Perspectives on Educating for Social Change,* she is currently completing her book, *Engendering Curriculum History* for Teachers College Press.

Nicholas Paley is an Associate Professor of Education at George Washington University. He is the author of *Finding*

Art's Place: Experiments in Contemporary Education and Culture and other writings, installations, and projects which explore relationships between artistic practice and the production of educational knowledge.

Bruce Wilson is a writer and practicing artist who also works as a substitute teacher in elementary schools in Sonoma County, California. His many research and writing projects examine issues of the collective unconscious and the spiritual aspects of human existence.

CHAPTER ONE

JANICE JIPSON
NICHOLAS PALEY

DAREDEVIL RESEARCH

RE-CREATING ANALYTIC PRACTICE

An Introduction

> "...the critical importance of the individual path in
> the making of a social whole."
>> Herbert Muschamp, *Room for Imagination*
>> *in a Temple of Reason*

Several women approach an elevated stage as pompous
music plays. Wearing dark robes reminiscent of graduation
ceremonial regalia and colorful feathered Mardi gras
masks, the women enact a familiar scene from a daytime
talk show program. The dramatic routine focuses on the
testimonials of academic women who speak of how they
have struggled to transit academic terrain and have been
duly transformed into academic vampires. The hostess
interrogates each woman in turn about her submission to
academic authority and her subsequent reincarnation into
the predatory world of higher education. At periodic inter-
vals, a woman stands before the panel to enthusiastically
promote various fictitious consumer products, adding a
word from the "corporate sponsors" (Ford, Rains, Collay, &
Dunlap, 1994).

A roundtable presentation begins, but none of the scheduled speakers is present. The conference table is empty except for an electronic tape machine connected by an external audio cable to a 3 inch micro-speaker. Next to the micro-speaker, a low, open container holds a neatly stacked arrangement of handouts. The presentation itself consists of a 45 minute audio sequence in which nothing is heard except an irregular, continuous clicking noise. On each of the handouts, the following statement is printed: "The presentation you hear is an electronic research per-formance. The transmission is an edited version of a 436 line study about teachers' selection of literature for use in classroom settings being entered onto an IBM Desktop Computer on March 25, 1995 between 12:47 and 2:32 p.m. EST. Installed as an *Art Slash Knowledge* (ASK) project, the presentation questions established protocols of analytic production/reception and systems that recirculate desire through the immediate, objectified consumption of knowl-edge" (Jipson & Paley, 1995).

A researcher displays a videotape segment from *Swiss Family Robinson* wherein a horde of invaders threatens the sanctity of the Robinson family home. His analysis is a rapid-fire series of multiple, conflicting interpretations of children's responses to the video segment. No single analy-sis is privileged. No generalizations are made. No conclu-sions are drawn from the data. No implications for future analysis are presented (Tobin, 1994).

What counts as research? What matters as data? What procedures are considered legitimate for the production of knowledge? What forms shape the making of explanations? What constitutes proof?

At first glance, responses to these kinds of questions seem so straightforward that the matter appears no more controversial than a closed case. Usually, the doing of research is engaging in problem-solving practice, a learned, ordered activity characterized—in large part—by the production of subject-object oppositions, discursive patterns, sequential, linear narratives, and objective analytic voice. The entire matter, however, seems more complex than this. At the moment, questions about the terms and propositions of research, and about ways of encoding experience in analytic form are currently attracting as much attention as any other issue in contemporary educational study.

While a considerable part of this attention is the result of a decade's sustained focus on the different, relative merits of quantitative and qualitative research models, a much more recent discussion (Donmoyer, 1996; Gitlin, 1994; McLaren & Giarelli, 1995; Stake, 1995) has been occasioned by an increasingly bold and spirited body of work that has erupted during the past several years across the analytic landscape. Provocatively also described as research, this newer work has jolted traditional notions of how to identify issues for inquiry, select modes of analysis, and inscribe "data" into transmittable form.

As forms of this newer kind of practice continue to erupt in multiple ways, in multiple locations, for multiple reasons, inside and outside the grids of defined research categories, the sphere of scholarly inquiry has become an extraordinarily animated site for a diverse and experimental analytic production by a number of thinkers not hesitant to situate inquiry in a vaster epistemological space.[1] Increasingly, this production has pushed beyond conventional formulations and has linked the construction of research knowledge to alternative models of representation including performance art, personal conversation, nonobjective artistic practice, asignifying presentation, journal entry, dream narrative, deep subjectivity, and fictional production.

This is a book about these kinds of experiments. By implication, it is also about what the artist Elizam Escobar

(1990) has called "the power of the imagination's struggle" (p. 86). More specifically still, it is about efforts to re-create structures and disclosures of knowledge that are responsive to, but unconstrained by, the weight of traditional research protocols. That we have chosen to collect examples of these kinds of experiments in book form reveals our sympathies with such explorations, as well as with the transformations that these efforts seek to effect within a complex pedagogical and critical field. This choice also clearly reveals our sympathies and affiliations with the voices of a growing number of educational thinkers, research workers, and cultural theorists who have established a powerful, differently-constituted set of imperatives for reconstructing the coordinates of analytic practice in the post-positive moment (Apple, 1986; Aronowitz & Giroux, 1991; Deleuze & Guattari, 1983; Greene, 1991, 1994; Lather, 1991).

Taken individually, we find these voices singularly compelling and personally important. As teachers of foundations and research courses at our respective universities, and as writers struggling to construct ways of redescribing knowledge in an independent, positive space, we have worked in similar manner, and, in many instances, have found our encounters with the ideas of these individuals integral to the development of our own collaborative research projects. Taken together, we are responsive to their shared, yet differently articulated orientations for reconstructing analytic practice in ways that create narratives—or even anti-narratives[2]—that demonstrate how "knowledge can be remapped, reterritorialized, and decentered" (Aronowitz & Giroux, 1991, p.119); that provide "imaginative resources for picturing difference" (Apple, 1986, p.178); that inscribe the "textual staging of knowledge" (Lather, 1991, p. 91) at angles to official objectives of analytic power; and that make real innovative patterns of disclosure beyond forms of "already constituted reason" (Greene, 1991, p. 122). We admire the immediacy of these articulations and their conceptual independence, and understand them as fundamental to the wider task of opening up research and critical practice to a heterogeneity, rather than to the reproduction of an already known world (Deleuze & Guattari, 1983, p. 55). We like how they open up zones of possibility for intellect and imagination to launch analytic projects into unexplored space.

The case for displaying these experimentations in book form and making their energies available to a wider audience can not be overstated. To us, their presence is the material evidence of the kinds of political and epistemological eruptions that have emerged along what Michel Foucault (1988) has analyzed as "fracture areas" (pp. 36-37) in systems of organized thought and discourse—fractures, he asserts, "which open up the space of freedom...of possible transformation" (p. 36).

We see these upheavals as political in that such practices raise questions about the status of pedagogic, representational, and research authority. Pulsing with power of individual imagination, they seem to force their way through the present densities of analytic production in efforts to articulate "why and how that-which-is might no longer be that-which-is" (Foucault, 1988, p. 36). The sense of "that-which-is" becomes the sense of what-can-be, always ready to just break loose. Trinh T. Minh-ha (1991) writes: "In the existing regime of frenzied 'discplinarization,' such breach in the regularity of the system constitutes the critical moment of disequilibrium and dis/illumination when Buddha may be defined as 'a cactus in the moonlight'" (p. 8). It is in these moments of "breach" and "disequilibrium," "dis/illumination" and what-can-be that the imaginative then may function as a powerful political force: the power of making and breaking, concealing and revealing, "learning and burning."[3]

We also consider these eruptions epistemological in that such practices provide concrete models of how meaning-making and interpretive exchange might be re-organized, or re-formulated—or even initially inscribed into an analytic existence that has long-repressed the kinds of experimental transmissions and exchanges of individuals educated in, but dissatisfied with, conventional analytic structures. To us, these kinds of imaginative re-arrangements are multiplicative in that they provide others similarly engaged in rethinking issues of research practice with examples of what many writers have viewed as the larger project of what it means to do research today: How, for instance, might one express "understanding" other than through the conventions of printed language? Or how might it be possible to represent a given "issue" in plastic or visual form? Or how might the imperatives of a research of commitment (Apple, Brennan, Burdell, Casey, & Zipen, 1995) find inscription through the power of poetic voice? "In a moment of decentering, then, of eroding authorities, of disappearing absolutes," Maxine Greene (1994) observes, "we have to discover new ways of going on.… to shape our narratives in ways that do not duplicate other narratives" (pp. 217, 218).

Inherent, though, in such non-imitative production and textual rearrangement are clearly issues of risk. Redescribing the dimensions of analytic power by engaging in independent research practice and by gathering together a number of these individual experiments in contemporary educational inquiry under the rubric of "daredevil research" involves, in very real terms, a kind of tightwire activity within the academy. The ideological and personal dare in producing such work is not negligible, and to venture this gamble is a creation that involves risks which imply, in no small part, changes in power relations. Choosing to take up the task of developing analytic practices that cross irregular, unexplored terrain rather than to reproduce arguments within the geometries of recognizable intellectual space is not usually an activity that accrues dividend in systems of mainstream academic exchange.

Making real Edward Said's (1983) imperative of exploring ways to construct "fully articulated program[s] of interference" in the "politics of interpretation" (p. 157) is often a critical challenge. Taking seriously Theresa de Lauretis' (1990) articulation of the frequent necessity of "leaving or giving up a place that is safe, that is 'home'— physically, emotionally, linguistically, epistemologically—for another place that is unknown and risky, that is not only emotionally but conceptually other..." (p. 138) is rarely viewed with geniality in the hierarchical interpretive tradition.

But shifts in ways of thinking are rarely neutral activities anyway. The emergence of difference frequently disturbs ordered systems which have defined protocols for thinking and talking, creating and doing over time. More often than not, articulations whose terms are "unknown and risky" confront power that has determined what is negative and positive intellectual space. Routinely theorized, rarely concretized, the expressiveness and unpredictability of the live imagination generate tensions within the landscape of scholarship. With a kind of electric clarity,[4] its energies crackle into existence—sometimes leaping over felt gaps in theory or practice—sometimes creating them. Currents of unregulated voltage surge across complicated terrain in unpredictable ways. Questions—many with no clear answers as yet—flare up: From what orientation did these experiments emerge? What power relations do they re/produce? Do all non-duplicative imaginations liberate? Which restrict? For whom and in what ways? Why certain "bold omissions" (Trinh, 1991, pp. 155-168) and "holes in the sound wall" (pp. 201-208) and not others? Which way now? These questions, and the risks taken in raising and/or producing responses to them, reflect both the very real possibilities—and predicaments—provoked by the experiments in this book.

But what constitutes a research that's identified as "daredevil"? In what ways is it distinguished from "conventional" research arrangements? What terms describe "re-creating analytic practice"? While the research projects gathered in this book clearly arise from varied individual motivations, needs, and historical and personal contexts, and while their existence seems to resist rather than reproduce categorization, we consider each of them to express one or more kinds of shifts in critical thinking—or instances of creative analytic practices—that can be identified and described. Imagine these shifts less as rigid categories, see these creative practices less as standards, and an opening for thinking about them is made. Perceive them less as a taxonomy for constructing a kind of unity and more like functions that cause only multiplicities (Deleuze & Guattari, 1983, pp. 1-5) and a sense of how we consider these experiments emerges. We intend no hierarchy when we state that, despite their diffuse and fugitive energies, we can now talk about the nature of these experiments more materially. We can try to describe the character of their shifts, the gestures of their creative practices more specifically.

Clearly, one of the most obvious instances of these shifts is that of a diminished orientation to the mechanics of traditional research grammar. Concerns with the procedural rules of hypothesis, conceptualization, data analysis, validity, replicability, generalizability, and proof have, in many of these experiments, been reinscribed in favor of a broader attention to indeterminate realities of producing knowledge. The implications of such a radical shift in epistemological orientation have led these researchers to explore issues of multiplicity, elasticity, ambiguity, and asignifying practice in the process of meaning-making. This interest is reflected in the exploration of terminology and research grammars that avoid the pre-established stabilizations of unitary thesis, discursive assertion, and linear construction in favor of arrangements that function as expressions unrelated to "transcendent ends" (Deleuze & Guattari, 1983, p. 50). Made from the moment (for the moment?), the grammatic velocities of a number of the experiments collected here suggest particularity and difference, not sequence or destiny. Their expressions are everyday and practical, not foundational and eternal (p. 53). Several other approaches develop analytic tensions by introducing modes of the allusive, the contradictory, the fragmentary, or the absent as fundamental to research practice—essential energies that communicate imagination's subversive force. In still other experiments, conventional notions of proof are no longer central to the formation of research intent and methodology. If such kinds of approaches "prove" anything at all, they perhaps "prove according to a different mode" (Derrida, cited in Ulmer, 1983, p. 94).

Closely related to issues of grammatical re-creation is the question "Why restrict experience to only certain analytic forms?" The imperatives of the discursive, objective tradition routinely mask the critical, generative power of this question by prescribing interpretive structures that periodize experience into beginnings, middles, and ends; that display knowledge from a singular, authoritative position; that employ "standard" language for critical work; and that obscure the existence of their own interpretation.[5] The models of representation in this book challenge these maskings, and express inquiry in multiple, unexpected form. Central to this move is a more diversified, polyphonous display of knowledge where, as Patti Lather (1991) has suggested:

> Data might be better conceived as the material for telling a story where the challenge becomes to generate a polyvalent data base that is used to *vivify* [original italics] interpretation as opposed to 'support' or 'prove'. Turning the text into a display and interaction among perspectives and presenting material rich enough to bear re-analysis in different ways bring the reader into the analysis via a dispersive impulse which fragments univocal authority. (p. 91)

Or, as bell hooks (1994) has articulated:

> I suggest that we do not necessarily need to hear and know what is stated in its entirety, that we do not need to 'master' or conquer the narrative as a whole, that we may know in fragments. I suggest that we may learn from spaces of silence as well as speech...." (p. 174)

These recommendations suggest multilayered research possibilities that explore visual and linguistic experimentations, productions long-repressed in the analytic economies of Western educational thought. Robert Donmoyer (1994) has named such interpretive possibilities "artistic modes of data display," and Hayden White (1978) has talked about using "impressionistic, expressionistic, surrealistic, and (perhaps) even actionist modes of representation for dramatizing the significance of data which [researchers] have uncovered but which all too frequently, they are prohibited from seriously contemplating as evidence" (pp. 47-48).

Another shift in creative analytic practice involves changes in research content. Determining that which is worth knowing and, thus, of being represented and analyzed in the research process has been traditionally located within domains of prediction, recurrence, and endurance. The worthiness of such knowledge has often been defined by its ability to replicate regularities in the social world. Categories of frequency, value, representativeness, and generalizability have had an obscuring effect on the determination of what is worth knowing. The repeated focus on these selective discourses as bases for research production may exclude categories of content that other educators have found vital: the unique, incidental, and emergent occurrences of lived experience and the significance of everyday life (Bateson, 1995; Grumet, 1991); the intimations of "*super*-ordinary" life and its expressions of dream, wonder, awe, mystery (Heiman, 1994; Mullen,

1994); the poetics of "the silent voice behind the talk" (Schratz, 1993, pp.71-124); the iconographies of popular culture (Aronowitz & Giroux, 1991); and the power of passion, eros, and the erotic (hooks, 1994; Lorde, 1978). Conventional analytic perspectives generally disallow the creation of knowledges that are indirect and impure, unexpected and multifocused, or exciting, sensual, and intensely autobiographic. Attention to the potential of these kinds of determinations may open educational research to differently "authorized" agendas which actualize George Spindler's (1982) suggestion for researchers to make the strange, familiar—and the familiar, strange.[6]

Still another element that distinguishes creative analytic practice involves the redefining of relationships within the processes of doing educational research. Traditional definitions have posited a finite, allowable range of relationships that clearly articulate separations between researcher and researched, between the subject, author and even sponsor or publisher. These distinctions, constructed in the cause of analytic "objectivity," have served "to remove, minimize, or make invisible [the researchers'] own cultural beliefs and practices, while simultaneously directing attention to the subjectivities, beliefs, and practices of [their] research subjects…." (Roman & Apple, 1990, p. 40). The examples of creative analytic practice in this book replace these "objective" positionings with multiple relationships which connect rather than separate the researcher and researched; which encourage a plurality of voices and narratives; which affirm a commitment to interactivity that is egalitarian and non-exploitative; and which promote reflexivity as a strategy shared by all participants in the research process. Related replacements include research practices questioning the ethics of conducting inquiry outside of one's own cultural or community experience; practices questioning researching "the other" at all; practices asserting that authentic depictions of subjective experience can only be generated through personal reflections on one's own lived experience; and practices which take as their subject the often intuitive examination of one's own ideas and beliefs.

Still one more (but never final) shift in re-creating analytic practice involves extending the limited structural and personal options made available to educational workers for doing (and living) research. This reframing of researcher agency and indentity is an acknowledgement, on one hand, of the limited theater for the transmission of knowledge (seminar, academic journal, professional meetings, scholarly books); and on the other, a liberation of self from the socially determined position as an educator-expert (teacher, researcher, advisor) whose role is traditionally defined as a transmitter of constructed knowledge within privileged academic venues, and as a professional separated from the audience and actualities of a culture. Alternate kinds of self and research projections that are multiple and diversified can clear openings for ways to move beyond commonplace analytic positions which often reduce sense-making to fixed systems. The representation of educational issues including—but not limited to—concerns about private/public, identity/image, freedom/control, may find potentially new and powerful realization through research creations by teacher-poets, pedagogue-artists, academic-performers, and scholar-activists who, individually and in collaboration, struggle to "pierce through all kinds of structuralist and historicist interpretations that either deny or impose roles," as they "decide how far she/he can go" (Escobar, 1994, p. 50).

Karen Anijar, in "To Go Where No Woman Has Wanted to Go Before: Lost in the Final Frontier" explores issues of pedagogy, truth, and value from a radical critical standpoint. (Re)visioning *Star Trek* as presented in the narratives of the Trekker teachers with whom she worked, Anijar examines how "the polysemic articulation of (new/old) values" creates a powerful language which incorporates the perception of change without changing. The translation of past categories allows the mythic to move into the present, positing conceptions of change, yet presenting a discourse that is grounded in "traditional" positivist premises. In taking seriously icons of the popular culture as subjects for critical analysis, Anijar explores analytic frontiers that are frequently overlooked or completely dismissed as having virtually nothing to contribute to sociocultural interpretation.

Two deeply personal, non-discursive explorations provoke questions about the place and politics (or their absence?) of the poetic voice in the research environment. Central to both are issues of representation and self-representation where both writers articulate their own conflicts with the realities of academic production/confinement in order to flourish educationally, artistically, and emotionally.

"Drop-Off/Pick-Up Panic" presents Deb Casey's poetic mediation on her own experiences as an academic/mother. Her brief rush of words, often one or two to a sentence, conveys the complex, perhaps contradictory activities of women who struggle to combine their careers and families in emotionally and psychologically meaningful ways. Her imagistic use of words suggesting abrupt, immediate disruption, reveal and document that parental reality in a manner unapproachable within traditional modes of academic discourse.

"Sonic Day" by Joan Montgomery Halford, provides a glimpse of the kind of social, institutional, and cultural soundings (poundings?) whose culmulative, "crashing" power obliterates individual voice. Ironically nameless, but forever officially numbered for reasons of "social security," Montgomery Halford's student strives for psychic air in a meaningless, numbing cultural and commercial ocean that's seemingly filled with every sound except that of her own voice.

In her essay, "Teenage Motherhood: Public Posing and Private Thoughts," Gunilla Holm arbitrarily pairs narrative excerpts from the personal journals of adolescent African-American women with photographs they took of each other as part of a school project. The juxtaposition of personal, and often painful, journalized reflections against the posed and stylized snapshot portraits of each participant graphically suggests the dramatic collision between projections of self and narratives of experience in the young women's lives. Holm's analysis of how attempts were made within the school to disallow the young women's activity underscores the exposed conflicts between appearance and experience, autonomy and authority, regime and respect.

Donald Blumenfeld-Jones and Thomas Barone address issues of what counts as research evidence and representation in "Interrupting the Sign: The Aesthetics of Research Texts." Extending the tradition that explores the connections between the arts and the educational research process, they raise questions about the function of form in uncovering or covering up understanding. Their columnar structuring of essay, their use of conversational analysis, musical score, and soliloquy, and their employment of stream of consciousness voice points to the varied material realities of research construction as well as sparking unexpected recognitions (or resistances) across the landscape of theory/practice, stability/multiplicity, research/textuality. Their juxtaposition of these different modes of representation reconfirms the importance of the aesthetic as a primary variable of both research activity and the research reading process.

In "Curriculum and Its Unconscious," Janice Jipson and Nicholas Paley work beyond traditions of narrative and integration in methodology and knowledge display as they are routinely formalized in educational contexts. Deliberately engaging only the method of chance to guide their selection of images/texts, they construct twelve visual/textual encounters that invite reading in open, non-linear field, and that activate the energies of the unconscious in the experience of meaning-making. By juxtaposing a series of statements which form no apparent curricular narrative with images arbitrarily representative of the Western artistic tradition, the authors explore a politics of non-objectivity and surrealist research practice. Their essay raises questions about method and thought when both are released from the conventions of logic in which curricular knowledge is typically expressed. It invites readers to consider what is perceived when no bureaucracies of top or bottom, left or right, first or last, subject or object are inscribed.

Drawing on feminist traditions of narrative and testimony, Chelsea Bailey's "A Place From Which To Speak: Stories of Memory, Crisis and Struggle from the Preschool Classroom" reflects on her experiences as a teacher of young children and thereby on the nature of early childhood, the interactions between children and teachers, and the social forces which shape the sites in which teachers live and work. Borrowing more from the discursive and textual strategies usually applied in literature and literary criticism than those from research with young children, she rethinks the ontological and representational foundations of early childhood theory. Challenging notions of the child as "other" inherent in psychological and education models of childhood, she examines the self-text she herself creates within the act of teaching. Her reflections of moments of rupture in her own teaching suggest cuts/continuities between theory and the actual lived experience of children and teachers.

In a rearranged conversation, "Th at dia log ue at ni ght," Janice Jipson and Bruce Wilson literally break thought apart. Zigzagging across time and place, twisting and breaking, pulling and shoving the lines of usual communication, they collide, resist and then re-form their personal dialogue against the incursions and interruptions of other voices, theories, images, and memories. Their puzzling display of a series of transcribed discussions suggests the multiplicity of cracks in narrative research structure and the chasms that separate thought, voice and meaning. Teetering at the edge of analysis and anarchy, their dialogue presents a research that is a fractured correspondence or a critique of analytic discourse invariably represented as linear, smooth, and complete.

In Nicholas Paley's essay, "Neither Literal Nor Conceptual," a series of rudimentary analytic fragments/images emerges out of the dark. Legible, yet frustrating to read, the minimal display of formalized and hand-formed texts, and the seemingly correspondent but not fully congruent manipulations of several of his past research projects question the boundaries that define research as ordered system, binary conception, and objective product. Based on forms of previously established meaning and methodologies, the rearranged essay provides multiple possibilities for readers to construct new meaning in a metaphoric field.

Petra Munro and Janice Jipson's print conversation "Deconstructing Wo/Mentoring: Diving Into the Abyss," pieces their shared reflections on five years of collaborative work into a dialogue reminiscent of the film scripts of popular movies such as *Boys on the Side* and *Thelma and Louise.* Adapting methodological practices used in traditional qualitative research, Jipson and Munro cut up seven hours of transcribed conversation into topical fragments and then patched them together thematically to create a new dialogue, one never actually heard, yet one which creates its own context and meaning. In constructing yet another version of their conversation and embedding their voices into the scripts of popular films, Munro and Jipson challenge accepted understandings of truth, confront methodological imperatives of representation, and call into question formal traditions of collaboration. In exploring the very nature of their relationship through the dialogic form of gossip, they create a generative research of possibility.

In working together to produce this book, we found ourselves struggling to open up spaces for the language of independent thought and individual imagination. We wondered at what point in the history of analytic time did institutional power completely devour these languages? When did inquiry become the slave of state legislation? "The state," the South African poet, Breyton Breytenbach (1993) writes,

> is a blind mirror that will steal your face. Writing that aims at transforming awareness can be about searching for the margins to stretch the limits...that is, subverting the hegemony, unhinging the unstoppable process of accretion and accumulation, rattling the skeleton and the empty bowl of the mind, taunting that powdered death called Respectability, keeping the cracks whistling, fighting for revolution against politics. (p. 17)[7]

The imperative for making writings that "stretch the limits" is everywhere, and yet how are they produced? In their essay, "Rhizome," Gilles Deleuze and Felix Guattari (1983) suggest a way. Avoid all orientations to organizing memory and central authority. Create outsides, mobilities, n dimensions:

> Write to the nth power, N - 1, write with slogans: Form rhizomes and not roots, never plant! Don't sow, forage! Be neither a One nor a Many, but multiplicities! Form a line, never a point! Speed transforms the point into a line. Be fast, even while standing still! Line of chance, line of hips, line of flight. Don't arouse the General in yourself! Not an exact idea, but just an idea (Godard). Have short term ideas...Be the Pink Panther, and let your loves be like the wasp and the orchid....(p. 57)

Might readers recognize in the experiments of re-creating analytic practice collected in this book something of the gestures of the Pink Panther? The loves of the wasp or the orchid? Or will they find instead that the mobilities expressed here, still not yet so aligned with chance and the inexact, only reimpose the memories of a known world?

Notes

1. See, for example, the recent and classic experiments in literature and the humanities such as Jacques Derrida's (1987) *The truth in painting*; Rachel Blau DuPlessis' (1990) *The pink guitar: Writing as feminist practice*; and John Cage's (1961) *Silence* and (1969) *A year from Monday*. In educational studies, see the annual Bergamo Conferences on Curriculum Theory and Classroom Practice, and more recently, the general symposium *Yes, but is it research?* at the meeting of the American Educational Research Association, New Orleans, LA, in March, 1994.

2. Or, as Deborah Britzman has provocatively named it: "non-narrative narrativity." Her paper, *On refusing explication: A non-narrative narrativity*, was presented at the meeting of the American Educational Research Association, New Orleans, LA, in March, 1994.

3. We bring forward here the term "learning and burning" from Tim Rollins, an artist/educator who has used this notion to refer to his and his students' (Kids of Survival) work at the Art and Knowledge Workshop in the South Bronx.

4. Octavio Paz (1990) has used a variation of this term to describe the energies of poetry and the poetic imagination in *The other voice: Essays on modern poetry*. The specific wording of Paz's version is found on p. 150.

5. We bring forward these notions from Patti Lather (1991) *Getting smart: Feminist pedagogy with/in the postmodern*.

6. According to Spindler, this notion was first discussed in Erickson, F. (1973). What makes school ethnography ethnographic? *Council on Anthropology and Education Newsletter, 2*, 10-19.

7. We build here on Breytenbach's (1993) ideas and wording of institutional power "devouring" (p. 17) the resources of the imaginative.

References

Apple, M. (1986). *Teachers and texts: A political economy of class and gender relations in education*. London: Routledge.

Apple, M., Brennan, M., Burdell, P., Casey, K., & Zipen, L. (1995, April). *Committed research: Methodological and substantive issues*. Paper presented at the meeting of the American Educational Research Association, San Francisco, CA.

Aronowitz, S., & Giroux, H. (1991). *Postmodern education: Politics, culture, and social criticism*. Minneapolis: University of Minnesota Press.

Bateson, M. (1995). *Peripheral visions: Learning along the way*. New York: Harper Collins.

Breytenbach, B. (1993, March 28). Why are writers always the last to know? *The New York Times Book Review*, 1, 15-17.

Britzman, D. (1994, March). *On refusing explication: A non-narrative narrativity*. Paper presented at the annual meeting of the American Educational Research Association, New Orleans, LA.

Cage, J. (1961). *Silence*. Middletown, CT: Wesleyan University Press.

Cage, J. (1969). *A year from Monday*. Middletown, CT: Wesleyan University Press.

de Lauretis, T. (1990). Eccentric subjects: Feminist theory

and historical consciousness. *Feminist Studies, 16*(1), 138.

Deleuze, G., & Guattari, F. (1983). Rhizome. *On the Line* (J. Johnson, Trans.). New York: Semi(o)texte.

Derrida, J. (1987). *The truth in painting*. Chicago: University of Chicago Press.

Donmoyer, R. (1994, April). *In their own words: A readers theater presentation of students' writing about writing and a discussion of the pros and cons of artistic modes of data display*. Paper presented at the meeting of the American Educational Research Association, New Orleans, LA.

Donmoyer, R. (1996). Educational research in an era of paradigm proliferation: What's a journal editor to do? *Educational Researcher, 25* (2), 19-25.

DuPlessis, R. (1990). *The pink guitar: Writing as feminist practice*. New York: Routledge.

Escobar, E. (1990). Art of liberation: A vision of freedom. In M. O'Brien & C. Little (Eds.), *ReImaging America: The arts of social change* (pp. 86-94). Philadelphia: New Society Publishers.

Escobar, E. (1994). The heuristic power of art. In C. Becker (Ed.), *The subversive imagination: Artists, society, and social responsibility* (pp. 35-54). New York: Routledge.

Ford, P., Rains, F., Collay, M., & Dunlap, D. (1994, April). *The academic vampire chronicles: A reader's theater on women in academia*. Paper presented at the meeting of the American Educational Research Association, New Orleans, LA.

Foucault, M. (1988). Critical theory/intellectual history. In

L. Kritzman (Ed. and Trans.), *Politics, philosophy, culture: Interviews and other writings, 1977-1984* (pp. 17-46). New York: Routledge.

Gitlin, A. (1994). *Power and method: Political activism and educational research*. New York: Routledge.

Greene, M. (1991). Blue guitars and the search for curriculum. In W. Schubert & G. Willis (Eds.), *Reflections from the heart of educational inquiry: Understanding curriculum and teaching through the arts* (pp. 107-122). Albany, NY: SUNY Albany Press.

Greene, M. (1994). Postmodernism and the crisis of representation. *English Education, 26* (4), 206-219 .

Grumet, M. (1991). Curriculum and the art of daily life. In W. Schubert & G. Willis (Eds.), *Reflections from the heart of educational inquiry: Understanding curriculum and teaching through the arts* (pp. 74-89). Albany, NY: SUNY Albany Press.

Heiman, J. (1994, May 28). Written commentary on an earlier version of this chapter.

hooks, b. (1994). *Teaching to transgress: Education as the practice of freedom*. New York: Routledge.

Jipson, J., & Paley, N. (1995, April). *Research, repetition, anti-memory*. Electronic research performance presented at the meeting of the American Educational Research Association, San Francisco, CA.

Lather, P. (1991). *Getting smart: Feminist research and pedagogy with/in the postmodern*. New York: Routledge.

Lorde, A. (1978). *Uses of the erotic. The erotic as power.* Freedom, CA: The Crossing Press.

McLaren, P., & Giarelli, J. (Eds.). (1995). *Critical theory and educational research*. Albany, NY: SUNY Albany Press.

Mullen, C. (1994). A narrative exploration of the self I dream. *Journal of Curriculum Studies*, *26* (3), 253-263.

Muschamp, H. (1996, May 12). Room for imagination in a temple of reason. *The New York Times,* H54.

Paz, O. (1990). *The other voice: Essays on modern poetry*. New York: Harcourt Brace Jovanovich.

Roman, L., & Apple, M. (1990). Is naturalism a move away from positivism? Materialist and feminist approaches to subjectivity in ethnographic research. In E. Eisner & A. Peshkin (Eds.), *Qualitative inquiry in education: The continuing debate* (pp. 38-73). New York: Teachers College Press.

Said, E. (1983). Opponents, audiences, constituencies and community. In H. Foster (Ed.), *The anti-aesthetic: Essays on postmodern culture* (pp. 135-159). Port Townsend, WA: Bay Press.

Schratz, M. (Ed.). (1993). *Qualitative voices in educational research*. Bristol, PA: The Falmer Press.

Spindler, G. (Ed.). (1982). *Doing the ethnography of schooling: Educational anthropology in action*. New York: Holt, Rhinehart, and Winston.

Stake, R. (1995). *The art of case study research*. Thousand Oaks, CA: Sage.

Trinh, M. (1991). *When the moon waxes red: Representation, gender and cultural politics*. New York: Routledge.

Tobin, J. (1994, September). *Chinese eyes: What we know, can't know, and perhaps can never know about children's understandings of media.* Paper presented at the meeting of the Fourth Interdisciplinary Conference on Reconceptualizing Early Childhood Education: Research, Theory, and Practice, Durham, NH.

Ulmer, G. (1983). The object of post-criticism. In H. Foster (Ed.), *The anti-aesthetic: Essays on postmodern culture* (pp. 83-110). Port Townsend, WA: Bay Press.

White, H. (1978). *Tropics of discourse.* Baltimore: Johns Hopkins University Press.

CHAPTER TWO

KAREN ANIJAR

TO GO WHERE NO WOMAN HAS WANTED TO GO BEFORE

LOST IN THE FINAL FRONTIER

Now, you know, give me a break! I don't know much about all
the rest of the world but Star Trek has got to be the best of it!
(from an interview with a Trekker)

It all began one Sunday afternoon last year. I had gone to
see *Star Trek 6* with my son Joshua, because I like *Star
Trek*; I really enjoy(ed) *Star Trek*. While we were watching
the show, I made a comment for Joshua's ears alone.
"Doesn't that look like Worf on the screen?" A man sitting
behind me in full Trek regalia (Vulcan ears, T-shirt, and
communicator pin) turned to me, and in the most conde-
scending tone said: "Don't you know about the Kittimer
massacre?" The intonation in his voice was so reproachful,
I felt as if I did not know the most fundamental of historical stories at the basis of the culture that I live in. After the
movie was over, I decided to feign ignorance, and strike
up some sort of discussion with the man. Being the great
conversationalist that I tend to be, I said: "Nice shirt you
have." He told me I ought to go to the local Star Trek store
and he gave me directions. So I went out of curiosity and
in search of new trinkets and baubles. I did not expect to
find in Greensboro, North Carolina, the most suburban of

cities, an "All America" City award winner, located in the midst of the Bible (or babble, depending on your perspective) belt, a haven for the Trek world. But there it was on High Point Road, and inside were tricorders, and tribbles, and a bulletin board with notices of Starship meetings, Star Fleet Meetings, Romulan clubs, and Klingon anthropological groups. I had to (out of curiosity), find the Trekkers. I wanted to find out what "this" was about. What had happened to my favorite program?

Theoretical Musings: Seeking Out New Life and Civilization (?)

> We shall never reach the real substantial roots of any given single utterance if we look for them in the confines of the single individual (person), even when that utterance concerns what appears to be the most private and intimate side of a person's life. (Bakhtin, 1984, p. 182)

Because the self is both contextual and contingent (Goffman, 1959; Vygotsky, 1987), there can be no "generic" teacher; thus, the teachers whose narratives are presented here can only impart a curriculum which is significantly shaped by a world view that utilizes Star Trek as its aegis. Central to my discussion is the notion that shared sets of concepts, statements and explanations are developed within cultural groups. These serve to create a consensual universe within which each group member feels at home, sheltered from areas of disagreement and incompatibility.

Research unfolds everywhere. The problem is not with the voices that speak, but with the ears the can not hear (Casey, 1995, p. 216). The day I went to see *Star Trek 6* I heard a language that may have been there all along, but I was not listening. Certainly, I had seen Star Trek posters, bumper stickers and T-shirts. The symbols meant nothing to me. I had conversations with teachers who loved Star Trek and spent hours discussing the programs. I only heard television. I wasn't listening for anything else. I did not understand that within the discussions of the program, a community had formed whose nexus was a television show.

Thus, my collection and analysis of Trekker/teacher narratives highlight the role of social "dialect" (Bakhtin, 1981), "collective subjective" (Gramsci, 1980), "general cultural repertoire" (Popular Memory Group, 1982), or "interpretive community" (Fish, 1980; Casey, 1993). The social self can only be understood in terms of relationship to the specific others with whom she is actually in conversation, and with reference to the interpretive traditions to which she has access (Casey, 1993, p. 1).

Communal concepts, statements and explanations or social representations are developed within groups. These serve to occasion a structure and a consensual universe within which each group member feels at home, sheltered from areas of disagreement and incompatibility. Whatever is said or done tends to confirm the accepted assumptions and meanings. Collective subjective behavior is characterized by the persistence of a mythological perception of the past in the form of social representations. The mythologized past serves a fundamental function in the promotion of group cohesiveness and group consciousness.

Trek exemplifies the notion that stock knowledge and typifications create a paramount reality that shapes and guides all social events (Schutz, 1967). The norms promulgated by the sense of "paramount reality" bestow a taken-for-grantedness in the social world in which Trek teachers interact. Stock knowledge and the development of an interpretive community is acquired through socialization within a common social and cultural world and becomes the only reality for the evocation of the social self within the Trek social universe. The presumption of a common world based on the television program, *Star Trek*, bonds Trekkers to one another and sustains the interpretive tradition.

It is quite extraordinary to realize that these teachers are employed in public schools, given the public rhetoric on education based on such a dramatically different ethos. Recent research suggests that there are other groups of teachers whose fundamental values do not correspond to those of the dominant discourse (Casey, 1993). The lack of national consensus on the purposes of American education is dramatically demonstrated by this kind of narrative research. Further, the very nature of our collective premises on the nature of American public education is brought into question by looking at narratives of teachers who gain their sense of affiliation with particular interpretive communities.

I seek the Trekkers! : A methodological "Tholian Web"

Trekkers do not overtly display their Trekness in all social settings. They acknowledge that their belief system is not understood by the "outside." So they only open up when they feel that the terrain is a safe space, removed from criticism that might be levelled at the extent of their involvement in the Trek community.

> Lichtenberg, Marshak, and Winston report that they have received hundred of letters from secret fans who are 'respectable solid citizens who know their family situations to be such that they dare not confess the depth of their feeling for Star Trek. They have tried, perhaps, and have run into such derision, teasing, or outright rage that they now feel compelled to hide their love like a secret vice.' (Jewett, 1977, p. 29)

They practice their religion in particular settings in particular fashions, yet all the while looking for other affiliates by a variety of means. Most of the time, however, they maintain their "professional" aura, while practicing Trek only in the embrace of other faithful.

> Half the professors at _____ College are Star Trek fans, but they won't tell you. They would never in a million years handle checks like this or talk about Star Fleet. But you let us have a Trek-O-Rama in town and they come out of the woodwork. My first Trek-O-Rama that I ever went to, now, I said, 'This is

ridiculous. I should never be doing this. Here I am a mature adult. Mature adults don't go in for comic book shows.' And that's all I thought a Trek-O-Rama was at the time. So I went. I sat in the back row, back seat, as far back in the corner as I could get. I said, 'I'm just going to sit here and watch.'

And in walks this grey-headed guy: 'Hey _____.' Uh huh, it was Judge _____. He's a Circuit Court judge. I said, 'Judge what are you doing here?' He said, 'I'm a Trek fan.' He said, 'I wanted to come and get some new material.'

Two men and a woman walked in. Attorneys from _____. They spent half a day at Trek-O-Rama. I saw this skinny character in a Star Trek uniform. He had to be 50 plus and the thing was, he looked familiar but of course in a Star Trek uniform you never recognize anybody, and I just kept watching him. And he came over, and I said, 'How you doing?' And he says: 'Hi _____.' And I'm going, 'huh.' Trying to place him. He's the doctor here in town.

But I sat there and I watched judges, lawyers, doctors; I watched all kinds of professionals. Professors from the college show up at a Trek-O-Rama involved with Star Trek. And they believe, and philosophically Star Trek has made a difference.

It is not hard to find Trekkers; you just need to learn how to look. I recall the Gnostic Christians used to place fish symbols on walls as a way to find the church. Trekkers do much the same thing. Their cars will have bumpers stickers, or they might have a license plate with NCC 1701 placed on board.

One afternoon, several weeks after the *Star Trek 6* experience, I was walking in the parking lot at the University of North Carolina-Greensboro and came upon a van that had the Star Fleet Emblem (as well as a painting of the Enterprise on its doors), and I left a note for the owner. The next day I received a phone call, was questioned on my knowledge of Trek (to discourage participation from the unfaithful), and invited to a meeting.

Subsequently, throughout the year, I have attended conventions, and meetings—not necessarily to seek out new life and new civilization—but to meet Star Trekkers, particularly Star Trekkers who were also teachers.

I was guided primarily through intuition that there was something going on above and beyond the surface veneer of the Trek-O-Ramas and Trek Cons. I was not specifically looking for data to inform a codified set of conceptualizations; rather, I allowed the narratives from the teachers to inform the theories utilized. This resonates with the work of Michael Burawoy (1990) who writes that, "…An effective strategy is, at first, literally to ignore the literature of theory…in order to insure that the emergence of categories will not be contaminated by concepts more suited to other areas" (p. 10).

This manner of research permitted me the freedom to experiment with a variety of different theories and modes of analysis, highlighting those areas in the analysis that may be anomalous to one body of theory but germane to another. Allowing the data to emerge and then providing theoretical as well as methodological justification for what is contained in the narrative allows a layer of intertextuality that would not be available to me if I was grounded in a preconceived particularistic theoretical construction. I donned my "Star Trek Next Generation" T-Shirt, (re)viewed the programs, and armed with a notepad, pencil, and tape player went off to the "final frontier."

The Trekkers Seek Members: "Phasers on Stun"

Recruitment for the various "Starships" and manifold permutations takes place in a variety of manners all insuring that both the privacy of those recruited is protected as well as insuring that the membership is knowledgeable (enlightened) about the treatises of Trek.

> They go to conventions and they set up a table like there is a science fiction comic book convention coming up called _____(city's name)-con, and I didn't find that deal interesting. I'm not interested in comic books, but they'll set up a table there and they'll put notices in the local papers in _____ and _____ saying that there's a meeting at this library at this date or whatever the building. And then through Star Fleet they get

referrals. So that if someone had heard about Star Fleet, but not the local ship, they become a Star Fleet member. And then there's a card that they fill out where they live and all that. And then Star Fleet says 'Okay. This person is nearby. You are going to contact him.'

Or as one very innovative Star Fleet member does:

(She shows checks.) They come from...I don't have it here. I will have to get it for you...You can't get them but from one place now. You know what happens when I write a check? Do you know the kind of attention I get with my check? I have a business card for the local ship, and so when somebody is interested, I give them a card. They call the captain and make arrangements to join. I have sent five or six people.

I was in _____ a couple of weeks ago and gave a man a check, and I gave him a card and said, 'You know...you and your local ship will be different here.' He says, 'I don't care. All I want to know is something about Star Fleet.'

You run into people all the time and you think: 'Well, gee! Shouldn't they know that there's a local ship? I assume everybody should know but then I realize I went for five years and didn't know there was a ship in this area or anything about Star Fleet.' So it's people, strange people, you know, businessmen, attorneys. I have an attorney that picked up one of my cards the other day. I do some public relations work for a local doctor and I had to drop some paper work off. And I was showing his secretary my checks. The attorney walked over and said: 'Oh, I want to get involved.' And I said, 'Okay,' and he said, 'Hey, look! I'm a Classic fan. Tell me more about Star Fleet.'[1]

The Trekkers who are teachers also engage in membership "drives" through a variety of means utilizing their positions within the public realm to procure members for their individual ships. One teacher explained to me in great detail how her daughter and her daughter's friends have meetings after school to study Trek. They question what she called "school things" from a variety of the characters' perspectives, coming up with solutions from the interpretive lens of each of the characters. The students learn Trek. They do problem solving via Trek; they then learn to articulate the discourse of Trek, and in the process, students are then recruited for Star Fleet, all the while "improving their grades," and "developing" what the teacher calls "critical thinking skills." There was an urgency in her voice when she told me:

> …One of our big problems in school today and it's even in the lower grades is depression. Teenagers getting depressed and taking their own lives…Star Trek has done a great deal to alleviate that by providing a possible future in which there are solutions…Star Trek is the only place where I can offer these children hope.

Utilizing what might be seen as guerrilla tactics, her role as teacher, as mother, and as Trekker overlap creating sense of zealousness and righteousness, or (forgive the Frederick Perls pun) "she knows, and therefore she does." She does it to save the children who are worthy of salvation, which in her role as teacher comes from the process of education (which she feels is often confused with schooling). The "role overlaps" allow her to maintain a veneer for both parents and administrators of the good teacher who takes it upon herself to have after-school and weekend sessions that focus on the often utilized phrase of "excellence."

Another Trekker teacher uses her own children in conjunction with the children who she teaches in order to obtain members for Star Fleet. Specifying specifically the type of student that is sought, she says:

> Well, my daughter had her annual picture taken in a Star Fleet uniform. She has recruited about eight students. All of them are ROTC naval students. Now we are not talking about a bunch of dumbbells. We are talking about straight "A" students, honor society students, [who] have been recruited into Star Fleet. In fact, we can't figure out why the dumbbells haven't figured out what's going on yet. But we have; we're not talking about below average students. We are talking about the sharpest aca-

demic science students available in Star Fleet. Because it's not fiction. It's not junk. It is something that they think they will see the beginnings of…

Who are the Trekkers (and what do they seek?):Hierarchy, hegemony, identity and intelligence

My own personal observations define the membership of Star Fleet as predominantly well-educated, Euro-American, white collar workers. To create a consensual community, others from similar backgrounds are most often sought for discipleship. The narratives of the teachers verify my ethnographic observations. Nevertheless, the homogeneity of the membership is re-defined under the rubric of the Trek philosophy which has been delineated for me by the Trek teachers:

> When one truly falls in love with the philosophy of Star Trek, there are no strangers in life, there are no prejudices in life, because there are none. Every sentient being has a right in Star Trek. That is not found in any other culture.

In seeking out the "best and the brightest" (and apparently the whitest) for membership/discipleship, the stratification system already embedded in the schools, and in the overall culture, is both rearticulated and recapitulated. In one narrative, the teacher invoked Martin Luther King as an exemplary Trekker, even postulating that Star Trek would be more widespread had he lived; in a subsequent paragraph, this person used the word "nigger"several times. In another narrative, a different teacher explained why he prefers the children in private schools as opposed to the students in the public schools. A third narrative postulated that the "poor" "are not open minded," and "are set in their ways." "You can be poor, but you don't have to be poor and dirty…It kills me…It doesn't take much to buy a bar of soap…Maybe that's why they are poor because they don't do anything to improve themselves."

With each story of stratification, with each bias mentioned, there was qualification which was then rearticulated in Trek terms, purporting the value of absolute equality within hierarchical terms. Hierarchy in varying definitions and manifestations is of tremendous consequence to the Trekkers.[2] The teachers as agents of socialization within the institution of schooling, in combination with their Trek world view, utilize both roles and therefore are able to envision and equate ability and intelligence within a synthesis of the Trek discourse. Three different teachers remark:

> The teenagers today…But, you know it makes a big difference in the way they behave. In the manner in which they conduct themselves with other people. Trek fans get along across the board with people much better. They tend less to violence as a solution to anything. They tend to think in terms of, it sounds strange, in terms of logic. You know, what is the solution? Is there a solution? They look for solutions rather than reacting to what's going on. And I love it..I would love to see a club in every high school.
>
> …The kids involved are different than the run of the mill kids.

> Now, I have an eight year old boy and he loves to play chess, and of course he loves to play "Nintendo" and all the rest of the junk too. But, he's very good at chess. And there is a book…one of the 60 Star Trek pocket books about a Klingon game that is very similar to chess. Now I read the book. I read it. But it is so far up here. It's like no way on Earth. But, this kid has read this book four times. So he went to a Vulcon and saw a three dimensional chess set like Spock plays. So he got interested in that. And now he is helping to develop a Klingon gambit game. Now this eight year old has that kind of intelligence. Trek is Trek.

Identity in Community: "If Anyone Knew"

I believe that we often assume that a professional identity is the over-riding community (in the naming of oneself, which is a political act), but we are actually a complex of many roles that overlap one another. Each person occupies many positions in a society and it is incumbent for the person to understand each frame of reference and adjust her responses to each community that she is involved with. As we interpret and rectify the norms and expectations contained in each situation through the complicated web of situationality, we select from a repertoire of that which is faithful the relevant group. We are constantly rectifying and recreating in response to each audience (Goffman, 1959). It is important to realize that roles are not only what we do, but each role defines who we are, at least for the moment in time that we play that role.

Even so, "a given sign community is constituted by contradictory and competing social interests.... Given signs are in fact subject to divergent ideological accents depending on the specific context of their usage—what Bakhtin terms the multi-accentuality of the social sign" (Gardiner, 1992, p. 16). With this in mind it is relatively easy to see why the community must protect its members from outsiders. The "faithful" realize that their views may be perceived of as "avant-garde" in what can be envisioned as a Bakhtinian "clash of accents." Members of the Trek community respect the privacy of the individual members, for they recognize that they might not be accepted in their respective fields if the extent of their involvement in the community was known. Anonymity was of tremendous importance to the teachers who so generously provided their narratives to me. "I'd get in a lot of trouble if someone [were] to know this were me....", said one of the teachers. In other words, the "clash of accents...is marked by a plethora of antagonistic discursive forms" (Gardiner, 1992, p. 16). The Trek community realized that the larger societal order considers Trekkers marginalized at best (i.e., the Saturday Night Live episode in which the Trekker is told by William Shatner, a.k.a. Captain Kirk, "to get a life") and recognizes the significance of anonymity.

The Trekkers ascribe a politically significant label to their quest for anonymity, relating it to, (indeed usurping) the voice of the gay community. The term used by the

Trekkers is "closet-ness." All of the narratives speak in terms and ascribe labels such as "closet-Trekkers" and "coming out of the closet."[3]

> We have a man here named _____. He's a newspaper columnist on TV. He's been in trouble recently. We get a lot of newsmen in trouble around here. But he's…he's a Trekker. Now he hasn't made a big deal about it yet. I don't know how much his general public knows that he's a Trekker. But I know that he's been through some rough times. I know that Star Trek has helped him through those rough times. He is supposed to be…In June, he will get his membership in Star Fleet, in our local ship here. Which will be nice. He has had a rough time of it, but his belief in the philosophy of Star Trek has helped him through. I think overall people who find Star Trek as a way of life…not yet but in the future…are people who are going to make a far better contribution to the communities in which they live. We don't just believe in Star Trek; we put it into practice…Things don't make sense in our day-to-day lives unless as a group we meet the philosophical aspects of Star Trek.

Commodification: "My communicator makes thirty Star Trek sounds!"

As I entered into the community, I entered into a world where television and pop culture had become not merely the medium of entertainment, but where the program and program text became the *raison d' être* for the disciples. I entered into a "secret society" where symbols and ability to articulate the discourse gained you access to the community. When I first entered the community I was asked if I "knew my Trek." The membership was suspicious. I was able to articulate enough of the discourse, having watched the show regularly for its twenty-seven year history, to be able to know or recall enough of the episodes to speak the language of Trek. Yet, I was told that in order to understand Trek I had to listen in the episodes for the "scriptural." One young man told me that if I studied the first movie carefully in conjunction with the "Concordance" I would be able upon the "seventh level to gain omniscience." I was also told that the Trek community uses the shows, books, movies, and fanzines as Baptists use Scripture. Pages and pages of my transcriptions contain cross-Trek references (i.e., in order to comprehend one aspect of Trek you must refer to another "text." "…If you haven't read Star Trek you need to because it will open your eyes to an entire culture that you would never see otherwise…").

It seems to me that the cross-referentiality serves several significant functions. At each of the conventions the sale of Star Trek paraphernalia was the highlight of the show. Each teacher interviewed showed me a myriad of Trek merchandising. One teacher showed me his key chain which made a cacophony of different Star Trek sounds; one teacher wrote me notes on Star Trek stationery; one woman showed me what she labeled as her "shrine room" (decorated in floor to ceiling Trek). A fourth teacher, after the interview concluded, asked me if I would like to get something to eat. We went to his car; he had a veritable library of Star Trek books inside, with his Star Trek tie strewn along the floorboard. He placed a tape in the player which, in quadraphonic stereo, blasted music from the canons (not of Pachelbel) of Star Fleet. When I arrived back home in Greensboro that evening I was so tired. Engaging my couch potato self, I turned on the television only to see a program on QVC based entirely on Star Trek merchandise.

The hegemonic metamessage of our time is that the commodity form is natural and inescapable. Our lives can only be well lived (or lived at all) through the purchase of particular commodities. Thus our major existential interest consists of maneuvering for eligibility to buy such commodities in the market. Further, we have been taught that it is right and just—ordained by history, human nature and God—that the means of life in all its forms be available only as commodities.

As the commodity form becomes a central part of culture, so culture becomes available for use in the interest of commodification as particular cultural items, as a source of commercial arguments, and as symbolic legitimation for the entire system. Culture and the commodity form become dialectically intertwined. Americans live in an overcommodified world, with needs that are generated in the interests of the market and that can be met only through the market. (Fjellman, 1992, p. 10)

At the community college where I teach, one of the administration officials told me the following story:

> There was this guy who came in to register for a woodworking class; he didn't seem like the woodworking type. I don't know why, he just didn't seem like the woodworking type...I asked him: 'Why do you want to register for this class?' He told me, 'To build a vault for all my Star Trek things. I am afraid that somebody might break into my apartment and steal my Star Trek things. I want to build a vault so big, and so safe, that nobody could ever break in to it.' He proceeded to describe in detail the size and shape of his vault, which seemed so large and cumbersome...I asked him, 'Well, how will you fit this in your apartment?...' I promise you...I was waiting for an answer...which was, I knew almost telepathically, that he was going to answer, 'I'll beam it.'

The primary function of cross-referentiality is part of the consumer culture and the commodification of life in a late capitalist economy (certainly Paramount and its licensees benefit). Yet, both secondary and tertiary functions are served as well: ownership creates discipleship, and demonstrates piety to what is elevated to the sacred realm. In addition the merchandise is used as a badge of identification pointing toward affiliation.

Technology and Theology meet in the South: "Beyond the Neutral Zone"

There is a belief in the literal interpretation of Trek. Although Star Trek consistently takes on themes of a "moral" nature, the program presents "morality" ensconced in detailed scientific jargon. The Prime Directive (a prohibition opposing interference with the social and physical evolution of any species) contains "technology in a moral and political framework" (Blair, 1979, p. 308). "Star Trek fought to create a wholly believable technology and a real universe" (Jewett, 1977, p. 18).

The believability factor sought after by the creators of the program was not merely created for the sake of technological babble or for "technology for its own sake" (Blair, 1979, p. 308); although, according to Blair, when dramatic effect came into conflict with drama, drama was to prevail. The Trekkers continually mention that the scientific and technological details in the program create an easily realizable universe.

> ...At least one crucial caveat is called for here. While exactitude and gadgetry are parts of science, they do not constitute the degree of scientific objectivity capable of calling one's own myths into question. The essence of the scientific outlook is a critical state of mind, which is willing to examine all dogmas, including those of science itself. Karl Popper, a major interpreter of science has even argued that '...what we call 'science' is differentiated from the older myths, not by being something different from a myth, but by being accompanied by a second order tradition—that of critically discussing the myth.'
>
> This is conspicuously lacking in Star Trek because mythical formulas so crucial to the plots are never called into question. Indeed, the myth of mythlessness ensures that they not even be acknowledged. Instead of a rigorously self-critical scientific outlook, Star Trek offers pseudo-empirisicism, an empirical veneer of gadgetry and crew talk applied to a mythical superstructure. (Jewett, 1977, p. 19)

The believability factor in Star Trek is essential to the program. "Things on Star Trek look right" (Tyrell, 1977, p. 712). If they did not look right, if they did not embody a technological fantasyland, the program content would not be as easily acceptable, or as easily assimilated.

> I don't think the things that they do are impossible, and they all come...you really listen...the stuff that they talk about...All that language that they use really is, you know, real scientific language. Which is kind of neat. It's not like they just make this stuff up. I just think its absolutely fascinating.

The technology utilized in the Star Trek show helps disguise the religious nature of the program by placing it in the language of empiricism and humanism which purports to castigate notions of traditional religion. (The Trekkers however are acutely aware that the nature of the program content for them is ultimately spiritual.) "Star Trek revitalizes American myths and places them into a futuristic quasi-scientific setting. In effect Star Trek takes our roots and disguises them as branches for some of us to cling to" (Tyrell, 1977, p. 712). According to Nelson (1976): "Technology as saviour has two important points: first, it is created by humans (so we can assume we can control it) and second, it has the vocabulary to sound convincing (whereas traditional Christian language no longer does)" (p. 144). Star Trek's reliance on technical jargon helps us substitute an antediluvian, Christian language for a rationalistic crypto-technological language, making assimilation of the same sort of principles savory and comfortable.

The death of Gene Roddenberry, the program's "Creator," has had particularistic ramifications in the structure of the community. He has been deified in an unusual phenomena of rearticulation via re-interpretation of the scriptural messages from Christian culture, in combination with the highly postmodern terrain of Trek. One teacher said:

> Gene Roddenberry died, but I use the word died loosely here. Gene Roddenberry died with a group of people present. He had written beyond his time. They, well everybody thinks he wasn't of this world, of the sixties, he was not just beyond his time.
>
> Gene was from another world. He was put here to prepare us for other worlds.

She then very forcefully voiced:

> I think that Gene Roddenberry was used as an instrument. I

don't think all that he did was his own…

Another teacher at the end of our six hour interview (which took place in a truck circling endlessly around her town) stated, in the same forceful manner as the previous renderings, that:

> I do firmly believe that God gave us Star Trek and Gene Roddenberry and all of Trekdom because I have never seen anything that would serve us better than Star Trek has.
>
> When Jesus spoke on the Sermon on the Mount and when he dealt with the Pharisees and the Sadducees or the religious leaders of his day, it is exactly what you face today with religious leaders and their prejudices against one another. The Pharisees wouldn't talk to the Sadducees, and neither would talk to the Essenes, and none of them had anything to do with Jesus because he was so different from their lifestyles.
>
> Now in Star Trek we have the fulfillment of all what Jesus said on the Sermon on the Mount. Because we believe in the brotherhood of mankind. And doing good to our neighbors developing our relationships with each other, and this is not Gene Roddenberry's philosophy. It was 2,000 years before him!
>
> I am as convinced as anybody can be that 2,000 years ago the Lord foresaw Star Trek and Gene Roddenberry. And that there would be those of us who would follow this belief even though it did not coincide with the beliefs of those around us in the religious world.
>
> I think our religious world…What do you call them…Pharisees or Baptists, whatever…We still have this little cubbyhole that we have to fit everything in. And Star Trek doesn't. Star Trek says, you're my brother whether you're black or white or red or yellow. Whether you believe in my lifestyle or a different lifestyle. And that comes from a Bible scholar!

All the teachers interviewed live in a five state region in what is commonly referred to as the "Deep South." The Trekker/teachers interviewed all have experienced alienation on some level with the traditional Christian church. The "South," or the South that defines itself as part of the Bible belt maintains an infrastructure of "belief." I have been told that "you can't be Southern without religious life being an important part of your life," so one religious tenant was traded for a seemingly differential belief, "the myth of mythlessness" (Jewett, 1977, p. 29). However, the belief, it would seem, is just as evangelical, and is based on the same ethos embedded in the fundamentalist discourse. According to the Trekkers, the organizational demographics of all the "fan organizations" demonstrate that the "South" has a larger following than the "North." Two teachers explain:

> They won't explore any other aspect; they'll live and die in that church with that one religion, with the one view. And that's all they care about. They don't want to find anything else. That's why I think it's really weird. The South has a real following for Star Trek. Maybe that's why they're so closet-y 'Cause they are trying to break off from this pattern. And yet they don't want to 'cause...the society down here says that's bad, so they do it in the closet...because that's their alternative to their religion that they are...force-fed.

> ...Being raised in the South, religion has always been black and white. You live in this box. You don't dance. You don't go to the movies. You don't watch television. And this guy over here is going to hell and you're not. And that's the only difference in the world. And this guy over here he's living in this little box and he's got the same kind of beliefs, and you're going to hell. And this one over here says you can't cut your hair and can't wear short sleeves and you can't wear this and you can't wear that and you're going to hell. In Star Trek now, there are Baptists, Methodists, Catholics, Jews, Protestants.

> ...Star Trek has made a difference in my life in the way I handle people and live with people across the board. Strangely enough, people who are totally involved in Star Trek are not prejudicial by race, by religion. In fact, how would you put it?

Although Trek would appear to be antithetical to religion, it is a religious ethos. Yet by existing in response to an old paradigm rather than positing a new one, Trek remains the antithesis to the thesis (in Trek pseudo-scientific terms, the "matter/anti-matter" dichotomy), trading off one set of beliefs for another set. Star Trek presents an alternative church. They don't have to announce or go to. They can have it right in their own little home every Saturday night.

Roddenberry himself was both a Southerner and raised in the Baptist church. He regularly elaborated about how and why he rebelled from Christianity. There is an old axiom that says that there is a fine line between love and hate, and it can be envisioned that indifference is the true opposite of either emotion, for it exists outside of the paradigm; it is not the flip side of the same coin. Roddenberry's religious sentiments clearly demonstrate the same ethos (i.e., responding to, rather than not responding at all). From an interview conducted for the *Humanist* magazine in April of 1991:

> My family was from the South. My mother was very religious. Every Sunday we went to church. Baptist church...I listened to the sermon, and I remember complete astonishment because what they were talking about were things that were just crazy. It was communion time, where you eat this wafer and are supposed to be eating the body of Christ and drinking his blood. My first impression was, This is a bunch of cannibals they've put me down among! For some time I puzzled over why they were saying these things, because the connection between what they were saying and reality was very tenuous. How the hell did Jesus become something to be eaten? I guess from that time it was clear to me that religion was largely non-sense—largely magical, superstitious things...I just couldn't see any point in adopting something which was obviously phony and superstitious...Santa Claus doesn't exist. Yes, I think back on it now that there were all sorts of reasons he could not exist and maybe have a little sadness that he is gone, but I think the same thing about Jesus and the Church (Roddenberry, cited in Alexander, 1991, p. 6).

In the same interview, Roddenberry further explains that:

> I was born into a supernatural world in which all my people—
> my family usually said, 'That is because God willed it,' or gave
> other supernatural explanations for whatever happened. When
> you confront those statements on their own, they clearly don't
> make sense. They are clearly wrong. You need a certain amount
> of proof to accept anything, and that proof was not forthcom-
> ing. (p. 8)

Max Weber "anticipated the advent of new and terrify-
ingly irrational gods in the minds of those who were to live
in the rational cage of modern society" (Luckmann, 1991,
p. 168). Secularization, institutionalization and bureaucrati-
zation of our culture did not cause religion to fade away;
religion, however, is placed under a "variety of disguises"
(p. 169).

In the episode "Who mourns for Adonis?," Kirk tells
Apollo that "We have outgrown you…You have asked for
what we can no longer give." He admits the time of the
gods is gone. (Jewett, 1977, p. 11) The episode attempts to
give a clear message that the era of myths is over and "science" could explain everything (including the presence of
gods). In Trek, philosophical constructs of "science"
(including the quasi-holy Trinity with Roddenberry, or
Spock at the head of the triangle[4]) take on the role of the
god. The truth/proof relationship in the Trek world ele-
vates science to a new religious order by castigating archa-
ic gods and elevating an Aristotelian notion of "truth" as
supreme. Yet the culturally salient infrastructural need for
a "truth," a provable truth, remains constant. The paramount order, the idealistic paradigm, does not present a
differing structure but rather builds on the same structure.
Therefore, there exists a firm grounding in dominant cultural themes which makes the program facilely discernible
for the disciples.

Between 1966–1968, seventy-nine original episodes of
the program Star Trek were produced. My sense surrounding the subsequent phenomena is that had the show
not gone off the air so abruptly, we would not see Trek

manifested in the same type of format, providing the same sentiments that it currently provides to its membership. Yet, the program did go off the air after three seasons. It was the fans who kept Trek alive by scripting their own stories and subsequently creating first a social group via the conventions and fan clubs, fanzines and slash-fanzines as well as creating a literary genre in novels based on the original show. The constant repeats in syndication gave Trek further impetus to be looked at as a scriptural, religious text. By the time the movies and the two new Trek shows were produced, Star Trek had become not only a way of life, not only a philosophical premise, but a dogmatic codified religion as well. The schools are but one way in which the religion is spread and converts are inducted into the belief system. Star Trek presents a reformulated scientific version of fundamentalism under the guise of a pop culture artifact that has been translated into a perceived "reality" on the part of the Trekker "collective subjective."

Truth, Justice and the Federation (American) Way

The themes in Trek act as personal exemplars in defining the ideals of the American experience (adventure?) in terms of "universally" equitable and legitimate ideology to be pursued by all people at all times.

> It is also highly democratic; it reflects the best of democratic ideals. So, if you want to take American ideals to their nth degree, I think that's where you'll find it.

> Well, it's American to the extent that it's democratic, it's our ideals of equality and tolerance. And everybody taking part. Yes, it's not just American in terms of who it would like to include and who it would like to appeal to, but it's, I think, if you take American ideals and take them to their end, that's it.

> Trek is Americanism/capitalism par excellence.

> The moral vision of Star Trek thus partakes of the spirit and rhetoric of Pax Americana. Its basic moral principle is zeal for its mission. This is in effect what authors Lichthenberg, Marshak

and Winston celebrate in their comprehensive fan book, *Star Trek Lives!* They affirm an admirable.... 'equality of moral stature' on the parts of Spock and Kirk. Each of them is that rarest of all things among men, a man of unbroken integrity...each remains dedicated to the striving, extravagantly willing to pay the price. But when one measures this moral quality against standards forbidding deceit, adultery, and violence, the lack of restraint is striking. What we have here is moral zeal attached solely to the mission and to their own vision of what amounts to the 'American Way.' It is a zeal transcending both due process and the moral code of the Federation's non-interference directive, which Kirk has sworn on pain of death to uphold. This directive is consistently broken in Star Trek episodes when 'necessary' for the fulfillment of the mission. (Jewett, 1977, p. 6)

Somehow the Trek world-view speaks a language that is so polysemic it resonates with people from all segments of the political spectrum. One contemporary, after reading an earlier version of this chapter, declared with anguish "We must recapture Trek for the left!" Indeed, much of Trek does profess a Kennedy-esque liberalism. Yet, as one of the Trekkers said "Trek provides whatever you need." Certainly it does! One of the Trekker teachers mentioned the "KKK types" who were in her local club; another teacher in comparing his "Klingon" group to other Klingon groups remarked on the proliferation of "Biker types" in most Klingon assemblages.

Nevertheless, on the part of the teachers interviewed; Trek's hegemonic rearticulation embraces and creates a new/same synthesis that recapitulates all the elements of stratification and "hidden curriculums" under a different gloss. The religion then optimistically believes that American goals and values and the Teflon republic ideals of contemporary America can be put into practice and can work. It enables the faithful to feel good about Mom, Apple pies, and Chevrolets. It produces a recapitulation of traditional orders and values because the future will be bright. The teachers seem to be inherently conservative and idealistic (in a utopian/nostalgic sense), believing that, through both Trek and teaching, they can encourage the "best" in America (and therefore the world, the galaxy and the universe). In other words, to the Trekkers "What has failed in American experience is nevertheless affirmed to be 'true' because it is depicted operating successfully in outer space" (Jewett, 1977, p. 32).

The Voyage Home

I have recently returned from the American Educational Research Association meeting in Atlanta. While there I went to see an exhibition at Sci-Tek, the Atlanta science museum entitled *Federation Science.* It is to be a traveling exhibition. Members of Star Fleet and other Trek clubs have donated their time and energies to help with the show. The show (again I remind myself) was held at a science museum—as if Trek has existed, or will exist. The exhibition was set up with actors from the shows explaining future science; there was a bridge set up, and there were several interactive projects. That may seem quite benign, but let us not forget that at the Smithsonian Institution's National Air and Space Museum, the Enterprise does sit next to the spirit of Saint Louis, as if it actually had flown! If the future is being invented via a television program that never existed, (as a political philosophical utopian world view, and as prophetic technology), then our future becomes limited and prescribed. The cyclical (re)creation of Star Trek looks forward in order to look back on what never was or will be. The future is being invented through Star Trek. The science exhibition presented inventions derived from the vision of the television show.

Star Trek displaces potentiality. The science exhibition demonstrated this. The teachers' narratives also point this out. Star Trek *will be,* because, if the face of the future is based on Trek, it is not open to the realm of possibility.

I don't think everybody realizes how involved Star Trek is in everyday life, in ordinary people...For instance, the diagnostic bed that is used in Emory University to monitor heart patients came from Star Trek. The hand-held UHM medical scanner has been on the market for 5 or 6 years now. Run it down the middle of your back and it can diagnose many problems: Star Trek!

Star Trek does not merely trade one metaphor for another and then subsequently shift the metaphor in terms of the hegemonic discourse. Witness the changes that occurred in the cultural acceptance of the Klingons into the monomyth as proud warriors in *The Next Generation*, and the creation of new enemies in a 1984-like enemy of the week that is reminiscent of our own interplay with friends and enemies in our own consciousness, for example, the Iraqis. Star Trek rearticulates the American myth by displacing the myth in a futuristic technological setting, disguising the myth, reaffirming a monomyth and discourse for those who otherwise might have been alienated from the metaphors of the original discourse.

Tyrell (1977) asserts that because television works on a non-reasoning, emotional level, there is no willed suspension of belief that needs to occur; it is the medium best suited to the creation of "mythos." Star Trek is exploitative on varying levels, but it clearly exploits the power of intimate communication that occurs between the individual and the television.

Star Trek's message of revitalized mythic narratives brought directly to the emotional needs of the viewer, engendered the feeling that the shows were more than escapist entertainment. They had meaning. That meaning transformed the 48 minute episodes into rituals and rituals being group creating, led to clubs and to the convention. (Tyrell, 1977, p. 712)

The Trekkers do not perceive the show as merely being a television show (as evidenced in the confusion between the "reality" of the day-to-day and the fantasy provided by the shows). Several of the teachers expressed experiencing anomie and isolation prior to being "saved" by Trek. "Trek fills a void in my life." The shows become canonical and philosophical/religious treatises on how one should live and how one should seek to live their lives. The clubs and conventions bring a sense of community together, further feeding on the sense of affiliation derived from involvement in the Trek world. The ritual of the conventions and meetings provides an entree and integration into an interpretive community. Individuals must feel like active participants in a community in order to experience a sense of affiliation; the authority of the ceremonious as a form of social integration can not come from a detached or anomistic position. Trekkers must live the "veracity" of the sanctioned rituals and myths in order to confirm their place in the larger symbolic order. This could not transpire under mythic and ritualistic conventions if there was not a withdrawal from the ordinary world into the realm of portentous cosmos (space) in which the life experience is intensified. This unusual symbiosis has ultimately transferred Trek into the terms of the apocalyptic:

> If you take Star Trek out of our society right now we won't have any answers to the future. We have nothing. There's a possibility there's a Vulcan someplace running around who is going to show up here with a friend and crash land in the lake. …Somebody's going to say that he'll come back in 40-50 years with a ship full of them. Now that's a possibility and that possibility can make the difference between death and life…

I have kept a running "press package" on Star Trek for a while now. What may seem innocuous or even fun on a surface level may have tremendous implications. I have read that Klingon is the most popular new language, and that it is being taught at several different universities. I have read articles about two year olds dressing up as Borgs and parading around at conventions where they learn to speak the language of Trek. There are Star Fleet academies of history, science, and engineering *ad nauseam*. The breadth of the material is exhaustive and exhausting!

It is everywhere but it is placed so as to make it all seem somewhat sporadic and innocent; it is presented in a way to make it appear to be superficial. I do not want to profess that a concerted conspiracy is in the making; that would be entirely too paranoid! *Yet*, I do know that everyone I have ever known is aware of Trek at some level, and that there are evidences of Trek within all segments of the culture. Even a space shuttle has been named "Enterprise" in honor of "the ship." Many of my friends label themselves as Trekkers. True, they do not exist within the boundaries of the sub-culture; nevertheless, the label is self-ascribed. When the pieces of this all begin to fit together, it becomes "science fiction" of the most paranoid sort (i.e., Pod People and Stepford Wives), for it is everywhere and it is constant. It comes from so many directions that we barely pay attention to it. It is in the malls, it is in magazines and newspapers; it is even self-referential via the mass media.

As I scratch the surface of Trek, I don't know what to make of all of this. Conspiracy theories dancing in my head, I try to sleep feeling compelled at night to "raise my shields" and place a "cloaking device" around my house, and around my child.[5] "Highly illogical" indeed! Nevertheless, there will be more Trekker teachers to be interviewed next week, and as I promise to maintain the "prime directive," I navigate ahead "Warp factor eight," for the "adventure has just begun"!

Notes

1. The Trekkers distinguish between the series via what seems to be a "commodified" play on words (stemming from Coca-Cola commercials). Yet, on another level the series are distinguished through a "classic" versus "romantic" typology. Regardless of the rationale, the different series are referred to as "Classic" (the show produced in the 60's) and "Next Gen" (the current show) and "DS9" (a Star Trek affiliated program). Trekkers categorize each other by questioning whether someone is a "Classic" or "Next Gen" fan.

2. The hierarchy present in Star Trek is also present in the organizations that derive their affiliations from the program(s). The organizations are para-military in style. One moves up the ranks by completing certain requirements and courses. However, the full implications of the connections between Trek and the military are just too large for the purviews of one chapter.

   I was told by one respondent that the hierarchy in Trek is also stratified along the lines of physical appearance. The teacher said that the "officers for the most part are dyke-like and the membership is obese."

3. Not only was "closet" used in the definitions describing types of Trekkers. Additionally, words such as "hard-core" and "soft-core" (fan) were present in the narratives as a descriptor. Further, throughout the narratives there was the phrase "respect for different lifestyles" what this ultimately "means" remains to be seen. The Trekkers all had varying definitions for the differences between the "old" term "Trekkie" and the "new" term "Trekker" ranging from "Trekkies" as dilettantes, to "Trekkies" as the "nut cases," to "Trekkies" as "60's sort of people."

4. Salvation was experienced through Trek in varying forms. One woman was saved through Trek by her psychiatrist while recuperating from a nervous breakdown. Death as well could be overcome by salvation embedded in the Trek "religion." I cite the following narrative passage:

   Well I have this friend who is dying of cancer. Her greatest wish in the world was that she meet George Takei. So, he came here…He went to see her and they talked privately, Nobody was allowed in, just the two of them for about an hour. When he left, he was crying, and she had the most beautiful smile on her face. And I said: 'What did he say?' She said, 'Oh, he said a lot of important things. But to my mind the most important one was he said I'm not going to die, I am just going to be transported to another lifestyle.' She said 'that's all it took' because she said: 'I'm not worried anymore because I know when I go I'll just be transported into another lifestyle. I'll warp in space and there I'll be.' She says 'George promised to see me on the other side.' She's young! She's thirty two; she has two children. If she sees the end of the year she'll be lucky! They give her no hope at all! But, the idea that death isn't a dread, it's just being transported into another universe, another lifestyle. That's what Gene Rodenberry has given us!

This passage does not exist in isolation, for several of the other Trekkers interviewed believe in immortality due to the constant cyclical nature of time, which transports the individual to another dimension. Behavioral and physical alterations exist as well; the literature describes a young man changing his name to Spock and the dressing in the manner of his saviour.

5. As much as I wanted to shield my child from the "effects" of a deep involvement in Trek, I also would like to express my thanks to him. Joshua Asher Anijar assisted me in a brainstorming session looking for Trek phrases that would be of use in creating this chapter. I would also like to express my gratitude to my friend and mentor, Kathleen Casey for her editorial assistance.

References

Alexander, D. (1991). Gene Roddenberry: Writer, producer, philosopher. *Humanist, 51* (2), 50-38.

Bakhtin, M. (1981). *The dialogic imagination.* (C. Emerson & M. Holquist, Trans.). Austin: University of Texas Press.

Blair, K. (1979). *Meaning in Star Trek.* New York: Penguin.

Burawoy, M. (1991). *Ethnography unbound: Power and resistance in the modern metropolis.* California: University of California Press.

Casey, K. (1995). New narrative research in education. *Review of Reseach in Education, 21,* 211-253.

Casey, K. (1993). *I answer with my life.* New York: Routledge.

Clark, K., & Holquist, M. (1984). *Mikhail Bakhtin.* Cambridge: Harvard University Press.

Fish, S. (1980). *Is there a text in this class?: The authority of interpretive communities.* Cambridge: Harvard University Press.

Fjellman, S. (1992). *Vinyl leaves: Walt Disney World and America.* Boulder: Westview Press.

Gardiner, M. (1992). *The dialogics of critique: M.M. Bakhtin and the theory of ideology.* London: Routledge.

Goffman, E. (1959). *The presentation of self in everyday life.* New York: Doubleday.

Gramsci, A. (1980). *Selections from the prison notebooks of Antonio Gramsci*. (Q. Hoare & G.N. Smith, Trans.). New York: International Publishers.

Jewett, M. (1977). *The American monomyth*. Garden City: Anchor Press.

Luckmann, B. (1991). In Bourdieu, P. and Coleman, S (Eds.). *Social theory for a changing society*. New York: Westview Press.

Popular Memory Group. (1982). Popular memory: Theory, politics, method. In Johnson, R., McCellenan, G., Schwarz, B., & Sutton, D. (Eds.), *Making histories*. London: Hutchison.

Schutz, A. (1967). *The phenomenology of the social world*. Illinois: Northwestern University Press.

Tyrell, W.B. (1977). Star Trek as myth and television as mythmaker. *Journal of Popular Culture, 10* (4), 710-720.

Vygotsky, L. (1961). *Thought and language*. New York: Simon and Schuster.

CHAPTER THREE

DEB CASEY

DROP-OFF/ PICK-UP PANIC

ZOOOOM: morning frenzy, the held-breath beginning to each day. (Zip past the entire get-up, dress-feed-comb/brush-assemble struggle, the tension between adults as to who is doing what and who isn't.) BEGIN at the car: load, fasten, dash back for forgotten items. Check watch: two minutes past the sure parking spot. Accelerate. Stay calm. Sing, babble, wiggle, jounce, offer a finger to chew, look at the "Look" commands: back sideways; DRIVE. Five miles to campus. PARK. (First spot easy.) Unbelt, gather children (stay close! to the oldest), deliver one: sign in, situate, converse with Lead Teacher (casual mother), glance to clock, OOOPS! Got to go…Be thankful: almost past the tearful good-byes with this daughter. RESITUATE: baby into seat (again), kiss the sweet lips, eager eyes, (careful not to bend eyes backward in haste). Turn around. Now the real struggle. Twenty minutes gone in that drop-off (and the center opens no earlier!). Circle. Lot after lot. Seethe. No parking. No options—no good options. Give up. PARK on the fringe. Prepare for the hike. Gather bags, umbrella, baby stuff, books. Adjust Baby in the front pack, distribute weight. Stride! (And be thankful the umbrella isn't necessary, no hand left.) Trudge. DELIVER baby to grad-student in father's office. (Take advantage of his morning-empty space.) Whisk out baby decor: padded play place, fur, jump-seat, chewables. Nurse. Insistently: here. Now. Greet caretaker. Make fast small-talk. Say good-byes. Breathe—no not yet. Ignore the sudden squawk, tears of a baby who wants you. No, don't: acknowledge the uneasiness. Return. Console. Promise. Leave again. NOW breathe. Find a bathroom. Forget it. Late. Run. (Forget too figuring how on earth to regroup bodies with the car, where it is compared to all three of our stations. Skip the logistics of breast feeding connections and so on. Get to the day's close.) DEPARTURE: Get edgy as meeting runs late. Fidget. Lose all train of thought. (May as well be gone, but don't dare walk out.) Try not to be obvious as you pack-up, already overdue. Dash across the quad, and up three flights (fast!), present the breast, FEED her, hear her contented warble, relax, smooth her moist cheek, soft fontanel, marvel again: how wide her feed-me-mouth glomps around the nipple (See: we working mothers are not oblivious), keep her attached as you try to move smoothly, quickly, (the easy minute up), gather her pieces. Sweater her snug, hug closely as you run to the car, urging all the bulk of you to advance a bit faster, fearing you'll find your older daughter parked on the curb: "her time was up." Don't exaggerate. No guilt: you called explaining, think no more of it. Get to the car. Strap Baby in. Try to hush her yelps. Promise (again): soon… Remember what you should have brought home from the office. Try not to catch your mind sliding forward, backward. Don't think how what you'd like is a drink. A moment… Watch the road, shift, sing, juggle, jiggle, finger-rub the baby's gums. Zoom. Grab Baby (gently!): up and over (watch the head). Find Older Daughter. Apologize to lead Teacher. Concentrate on this reunion time: focus—while urging Daughter toward her cubby and out of the action. (And don't wrinkle the painting.) Keep Baby from the breast position temptation. Give-up: sling Baby over hip, connect to nipple, button Older Daughter's sweater, one-handed, gather the other drawings, praise (sincerely), pat, burp, sign-out (Don't forget!), get them out and loaded (again) into the car and belted and grinning, or grumbling (whatever), DRIVE. Sing. (What's in the fridge?) Shift.

"Drop-Off/Pick-Up Panic" first appeared as "(Justification) Drop-Off/Pick-Up Panic" in CALYX, A Journal of Art and Literature By Women. ©1990. Reprinted by permission.

JOAN MONTGOMERY HALFORD

SONIC DAY

U.S. Public High School Student
199-44-6037

Velvet ethereal voices,
      swirling,
         fading ...
          ALARMING BUZZ.

Sleep-deprived kitchen voices. Hurried, humming tires.

Cacophony. Voices in industrial tile corridors, administrators' realms.
Voice y voz et voix. Publicly announced.

Voices haltingly sweet, caustically harsh, monotonously ambivalent,
      resolutely authoritarian.
Delivering trivialities/mimicries/emotions/technicalities.

Intertwining, drumming, numbing, assaulting, ascending, crashing.

Sound waves flattening into meaningless voids.

Voices slic.ed.by.the.stac.ca.to.of.ar.ti.fi.ci.al.bells.

Home.   No voices.

TV voices, thrilled to discuss glass cleaner! Snack food! Beer!
Mutual funds!

Stereo voices pleading—for sex, love, death, and understanding.

Telephone-modulated voices with similar pitch, timbre, and angst.

Exhausted evening voices. Older voices requesting household help, logistical information, summaries of daily activity.

One's own VOICE? Drowned.

Return to dreambeat.

CHAPTER FOUR

TEENAGE MOTHERHOOD

PUBLIC POSING AND PRIVATE THOUGHTS

This photo essay is based on photographs taken by adolescent girls, students in a school for pregnant and parenting girls. Provided with photography equipment and invited to shoot whatever they wished, the girls took photographs that affirmed their sexuality and presented a very public portrait of themselves via explicit posing. The private side these girls chose to reveal is presented through excerpts of poems and autobiographies written by the girls, and through interview excerpts. These images stand in contrast to the school's program which, fixed upon traditional subject matter and patterns of instruction, ignored and excluded the girls' private lives and sexuality. Invited to do so, the girls present their identities and realities as pregnant or parenting young women through the presentation of these public and private images.

(The quotes on each page are not the words of the person in the photograph on that page, but are drawn from the other girls in the school.)

I'm still young even though I do have a baby. I'm not grown yet. That's why I just stay with my mom until I finish high school.

Basically I just want to be successful.... Basically, I want to stay out of trouble. Just not getting more babies, that's for sure. I just take it one step at a time and stay away from all the bad stuff, try and do all the good stuff so I can set an example for my son.

When I was born my father didn't claim me cause he didn't want to pay child support. I don't know why my mother let me know who he was—he didn't claim me.

I don't have friends right now. Can't trust nobody out there.
They turn on you and stuff. They hit you and stuff like that.

I'm scared to death. I mean I'm just scared it's going to hurt so bad cause like some of the girls that's already had their baby, they tell me their little horror stories and I be so terrified. Oh no, I don't want to hurt that bad. That's the only thing I really fear, the delivery, cause I'm scared it's just gonna hurt, hurt, hurt.

I was 13 turning 14 when I had my oldest. And I was 17 when I had my youngest. The first time I wanted to get pregnant, the second time I didn't so much want to be pregnant, but it just happened. It was my responsibility and I'm just gonna have to take care of her.

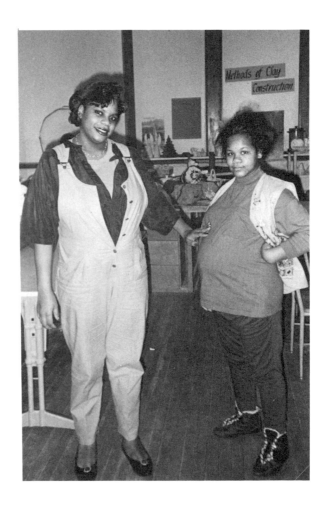

I felt I was staying with my grandparents and I couldn't go anywhere, I couldn't be outside. I couldn't be with my friends and you know I felt that they didn't love me and I said I wanted something that I can love and that will love me back. And so, after I met Malcolm, their daddy, that's when I decided to have Anthony, then we had Latoya.

Men talk nasty and stuff. And some of them act stupid. They don't really take things seriously. They like to play around too much. I think most of them are lazy. I mean they like you to do things for them, they don't do nothing for themselves. They like you to cook for them. I just won't do it for them, just let them suffer until they know how to do it themselves.

The safest thing I can do is not have sex. I can't take the pills cause they make me sick. I do use condoms, them things they break. You know, the safest thing I could do is just not have it.

TWO DIFFERENT FEELINGS

I love her very much.
>*My life has been put on hold.*
She is so very beautiful.
>*I want to do my own thing.*
Her smiles make me laugh.
>*I miss my friends.*
She learns things every day.
>*I have to work harder in school now.*
I love to dress her up.
>*I want to spend my money foolishly.*

I just go to school and go home and clean up and go to sleep and eat. We be at church on Sunday. Then after church I come home and go to sleep. Then I wake back up and eat, then I go back to sleep.

I was mad. I still don't want no other baby, but it's here now so I can't stop it. I was crying and I was scared to tell my mother. Cause some people ain't ready to be a parent. I know I'm not. I wasn't thinking of having one now, not now. I could do without having kids.

Men are men. They're the same—demanding, they want a lot, they expect a lot from women without doing anything themselves. Do this, do that, cook my food, put my clothes away, take my shoes off. I don't know, they're lazy, they're lazy.

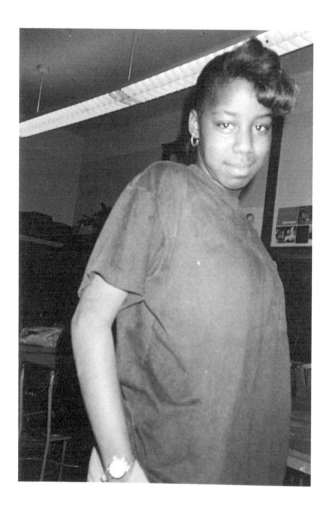

Before I had my baby I was lonely. Since I've had my son I'm not lonely. Not at all.

I'm sometimes funny, sometimes stern, sometimes mean and other times just myself.

I've been in foster homes cause we had problems in our family. Dealing with my father, he liked to do bad things to girls. You know what I'm taking about.

LOVE

It is wonderful to be loved.
The color of love is red.
It makes me feel like I am somebody in the world.
Love makes me as soft as a dove.
I feel like I'm being cared about.
I feel bright when I'm loved.
I feel warm when I'm loved.
I don't fight when I'm loved.
It is wonderful to be loved.

I can work harder, I just don't come to school like I'm supposed to. Because half the time my oldest boy probably be sick or my youngest daughter. They take turns getting sick so I stay out of school and make them better.

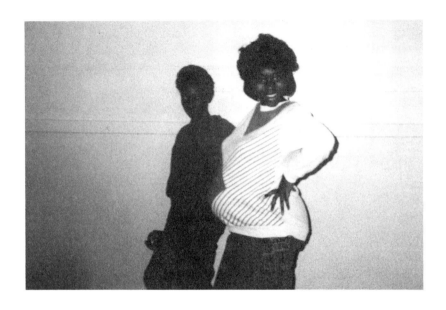

*I get **ADC**, but I really been looking for a job cause I rather have a job than be on **ADC** cause I rather support myself. I don't like for nobody to support me but myself. Me and my kids.*

You know, my grandmother loves me to death, I don't know why though.

CHAPTER FIVE

DONALD S. BLUMENFELD-JONES
THOMAS E. BARONE

INTERRUPTING THE SIGN

THE AESTHETICS OF RESEARCH TEXTS

In the last 20 years the idea of relating the practices of research and art has been developing steadily. Pioneering work in this area was done by Eisner (1975, 1977) and his students (Vallance, 1975; McCutcheon, 1976; Barone, 1978; see also Barone & Eisner, in press). A recent issue of *Educational Theory* (Bresler, 1995), was devoted almost entirely to the arts, knowledge and education with a special focus upon research. Reader's theater presentations of research at conferences has been on the rise over the last several years (Trousdale, Adams, Jacobs, Munro, & Quinn, 1994; Donmoyer, 1989, 1994; Sears, 1989). At AERA 1995 a special session was devoted to the use of arts disciplines in presenting research (Blumenfeld–Jones, Donmoyer,

LINEAR CHRONOLOGICAL

One format, the linear chronological, is the initial form which emerges from the work of a transcriber, and the form most often displayed in ethnographic research. In a sense it is an "empty" form, waiting to be filled with analytic intention. This format portrays the conversation as a series of unfolding topics moving smoothly through time. Hidden from view are the social processes of negotiation and recursion which inevitably occur throughout the conversation. This masking links to the dominant cultural theme of individualism, the privileging of the voice of each respondent as an isolate. Moreover, each respondent is reduced to being a reactant to the interviewer. Notice:

N1: So, with DF's class, we're

Yennie-Donmoyer, Gabella, Kinzer, Flinders, Rossman, & Reynolds, 1995). Jeffers (1993) also made aesthetics a central referent for thinking about doing research. In this essay we contribute to thinking about the salience of the arts to the educational research process, especially as they relate to analysis and disclosure of research findings. Specifically, we are concerned with relationships between data display and forms of expression.

The linkage between art and data display is not casual. Indeed, data display may be a form of concrete poetry that attempts to teach the reader about the findings of an investigation. M.C. Richards (1962) states that in the writing of poetry "everything matters" (p.81). "The spelling, the position on the page, the typography; the beat of the breath, the division of syllables, loudness and softness, rhythm. All these elements of form, graphic and sonorous, help to depict the experience. They are the embodiment" (p.81). This means that no aesthetic possibilities exist until words become embodied in specific forms. Care must therefore be taken with the embodiment. And so the poet labors over aesthetic choices of form in

talking about language and how language is affecting what—what kids learn or anybody learns. And the writing, the oral, the reading, how important it is; and the attitudes we have are important. And so we're looking—it seems like we have a—a certain focus that might, may or—that you can remove from yourself or you don't have to remove from yourself. You can make it more personal. Donald's class, the contrast, is—it seems like—it seems like we were dealing more with attitudes, with the attitude part of DF's class because of how we see things in working with other people, you know, in community. I've adjusted some—some of my outlooks on people, like T. I thought, "Well, T probably wouldn't like me (T laughs)." And then I − the other (T overlaps with N1:"Why?") day when we worked—(answers T: "I don't know. I just had the idea you didn't like me.") So I thought, "Well, I'm going to test this out." So then we worked—boy, T and I, we got together, and we did things, a couple of things. And, boy, you know, I—I guess I was wrong about T and I was telling F about that, "I was wrong about her." She has—you know, it's my eye—it was my perception, you know. I was seeing something that wasn't there. And I just wonder, "Well, how many other times have I done that?" You know, so it just

order to best represent her thoughts.

Much more is at stake than just unfolding artistic intention through form. Buber (1970) noted, "This is the eternal origin of art that a human being confronts a form that wants to become a work through him [sic]...[The] deed that a man [sic] does with his whole being...involves a sacrifice... The sacrifice: infinite possibility is surrendered on the altar of the form" (p. 60). The form, for Buber, is twofold: the Thou of inner sight and intuition and the materiality of the art piece, the physical form which is the limited representation of that inner form. This limitation, however, carries the ultimate value for in the act of forming is "discovery" (Buber, p.61). The act of forming brings to life what it is we can know and express.

What can be said for poetry holds true for educational research as well. There, too, form and format will both tell us what we can know and enable us to express what we have learned.

Form and Expression In Research Reporting and Analysis

When educational research is reported in a journal or conference proposal, it is canoni-

seemed like it was an easier, more protective place to be able to talk and really say something, and you—I don't know what other people thought about me, or but—but then I—I didn't seem to worry about that as much in our classes. And like it's easier to talk to everybody now for me, you know, it's a lot easier.

Dr. DBJ: Did you feel that—in—in these two classes when we're talking about who should have the floor—do you feel that, um, it changed you somehow?

B: Uh, (intake of breath) I kind of got the—I got the feeling—and I stopped and I probably still have a little bit of it, that (pause) you're not suppose to control the floor—I mean not control the floor, because when I was in Tom's class—not Tom's—DG's' class last year, I remember asking a question and getting so flounced up in the words, and I said, "Just forget it." And DG said, "Wait a minute, wait a minute, try it, and we'll work it through." And I've gotten a lot more verbal this semester, probably because I—it's making sense, and I'm excited about getting through, and—and that kind of stuff. But after that class, you know, like I had said before in DF's evaluation, that, maybe I should just sit back and absorb. But it's—(laughing voice) it's not how I learn, I want to ask the questions to get the—to make the connec-

cal that we employ the standard presentation format. The ubiquity of this format (introduction including the research question, literature review, methodology, data presentation, data discussion, conclusions and future prospects) lends the report an aura of common–sense and a certain status of validity. The format becomes a marker of the competence of the researcher, provides comfort through a sense of agreed upon norms. In Sausserian terms, we lose awareness of the effect of the signifier (textual form) upon the signified (textual content). While deconstruction may teach that signifier and signified are the same, when it comes to writing and reading research reports this lesson is often ignored.

The standard format may be considered a rhetorical device which not only lends credibility to the researcher but supports the truth–value of the report. Moreover, each segment of the report serves as a building block and the blocks are stacked so that the "conclusions" segment depends for its warrant upon previous sections. The form, in its linearity, drives the reader toward the stated "conclusions." The reader can glide

tions. And to me, asking the questions that I ask, it's not because I want to hear myself talk, and some people probably think, "God, there she goes again," you know. But I'm doing it for real, because this is my education. I got put in TDF for certain reasons, you know, pers—personal, you know, like I wrote in my ethics paper 'cause I was supposed to be here, and I'm gonna make the best of it. But after that class, I don't know, I kind of feel like, "Well, maybe I do outtalk everybody and that's not fair to them," or that stuff. But at the same—at the same flip side. I feel like, "Well, if they don't get it, then that's their problem (laughs)." So I don't know, I'm kind of on a debate. So everyone once in awhile when I notice that I could say something, like—like you said, I think, "Well, I know what I wanted to say, and it makes sense in this conversation." And sometimes I leave it at that, even though most people would say, you know, "I would think it would help them make those connections that I'm making." But I've been quieter (laughs). It wasn't that long ago, but I have been quieter in class. And, okay (upward lilt in her voice) (laughs).

N2: Right (overlapping B's last two words and laughter) I know for myself with the—I don't feel I changed at all with the experience of those two days in your

through the report, validate each section and move on without retrospection. The figures, tables and other kinds of data display are also rhetorical devices. They are meant to convey the data either in an efficient (e.g., through figures and tables) or supportive manner (e.g., through sections of transcript quotations or other kinds of direct representation). In all cases, the display is meant to legitimate the researcher's conclusions. The reader is primed to accept those conclusions as form (signifier) remains hidden from view.

One difficulty is that the political character of form is disguised. How so? Consider that research reported in an unconventional format is automatically suspect. A non–standard format prompts a careful search for the warrant of the report, indeed, militates against acceptance of the validity of the report. The authority of the text comes at the expense of the power of the reader to question the ramifications of the canonical textual form.

Readers bring commonsensical notions of form to bear upon research texts, even when these are essays or other less analytical, more literary

class. But, um, I do know that when I speak out it's because, hey, I want to make a connection, or I have a question, or I feel that my opinion is valid and warranted, I feel. Maybe—maybe it's not, but that doesn't really matter to me (laughs slightly),—and, and sometimes, you know, maybe it changes the scope of the conversation. But I know that when we— when we were in that class the people who do speak out a lot, or even sometimes infrequently like myself, it did seem like we weren't suppose to actually go on the floor. And it did seem like the people who never speak, it seemed like they were under intense pressure, and you could just feel it in the air. And that—I mean if you remember what BS1 said, she's not really close to anyone and she doesn't want to be. And once she's graduated, she's out of here, and she—she goes, "I'll probably never ever see you guys again, no matter what." So it's like, "Wow." So obviously this person doesn't want to speak up in class, (pause and downward turn of voice tone and volume) for whatever reason. But I mean, I don't—I—I know nothing about her obviously since she doesn't talk to anyone but (laughs)—(Others laugh).

T: But it did make sense, because she's planning on going back East—

N2: Yeah.

reports. A particular kind of "rounded out" Aristotelian format, with a beginning, middle and end, is commonplace. Most storytellers arrange their work in this familiar way, thereby failing to call attention to form. The reader's attention is thereby focused more on "content" than "form," more on the signified than the signifier. But, as with the example above, some writers, fictional and otherwise, break this taken-for-granted disposition. Alain Robbe-Grillet (1957), a French anti-novelist, is an example of a novelist who does so. Julia Kristeva's (1986) philosophical "Stabat Mater" presents two parallel and mutually intrusive columns of texts on the same page, prompting questions in the mind of the reader: Which should I read first? Should I alternate sentences? Where are the "natural" break-points where I might shift back and forth between columns? These sorts of questions arise out of the unconventional nature of the graphic display.

Of course, even with conventional texts the author cannot control for unforeseen needs of readers that can lead to playfulness with the text. For example a reader, wishing to know something before the

T: So that's—

N2: Well, it makes sense, but it's—it's weird how she doesn't want to get close.

T: She said she wouldn't ever see any of us again, which is probably true if she does go back to East (voice dropping in volume).

N1: You never know—

N2: Yeah.

F: —sittin' in that class made it a lot easier for me to speak too, because, uh, usually in classrooms you're facing forward. I usually sit in the front. The people behind me, I don't know who they are. And then I'll see 'em three weeks later and say, "Hi F, how did you like so and so?" I don't know who I'm talking to, because I've never seen their face. Sitting here in this circle like we do, or (pause) getting to know each other and then put a face on a name, I'd feel a lot freer in talking to you than I would ordinarily, because, you know, you don't want to talk to strangers. I— I don't like talking to strangers that much, especially a group of strangers. When you know 'em, it's like, "Well, I can talk to my friends, I can say what I want." If I slip and happen to—to use a word that I shouldn't use, they're not going to laugh at me or nuthin', they're just going to accept it as I am, because they know me.

N2: But also, on—like in your class and what F had said earlier, there's a lot of, uh, you know, off

author is ready to divulge it, may "skip ahead." Some readers rely upon an index to find only that information which is of interest. Or the end of an article may be read first. Or sections of an article may be read in reverse order. Indeed, a text is always potentially in free play and any reader can subvert the intentions of the author. As Stanley Fish (1980) informed us, there is, finally, no single text "in this class," no way to compel suspicious readers to obey the authority of the text.

Still, we recognize that, when an author employs novel formats, reader playfulness is encouraged rather than simply allowed. A telling anecdote illustrates the power of form for the making of meaning. In presenting a poster–session at AERA 1993 Donald Blumenfeld-Jones arrayed his "information" in three strips, horizontally, arranged with each section having a vertical orientation. More general ideas were at the top of the board and below was specific support through quotations from transcripts. The tops of the three vertical "strips" were not level. An initial dissonance was evidenced in the response of viewers. Almost all asked where to begin. Donald gave

the top of your head, or a lot of feeling and emotion, because people were dealing with their ethics and control, you know, should-a-person-speak-up issues that everyone has. And in DF's class, it was a lot more academic-wise with the, uh, you know: This is the material. Any questions or comments?

N2: I felt a lot better after it — and—and even if I didn't say that much, because I feel like—I don't trust very easily. And in there it felt like I could test something, and a couple of times I did test, because I wanted to find out, you know ...and that's the only way you can find out is by testing. And I was afraid maybe, maybe I'd be perceived as being aggressive or challenging or anything like that, and that's not my intent. My intent is to find out and to see, you know, like when I said that—when I said that about the red baiting, I knew that what I said was—was out of line, or not—I knew already what you meant, but I wanted to (slightly laughs)—I just felt like testing that. I just felt like—and I felt comfortable enough in that class and with you as the teacher that I didn't have to worry about, "Okay, you watch out, N. I'm going to watch out for you next time." And I felt that in other classes, so then I don't say anything. I'm quiet. I've never felt that comfortable in a class before, ever, to be able to say

the spectators "permission" to begin where they felt comfortable doing so. They began in different places. Most appeared delighted at the freedom afforded and the play provided. They did not even seem to notice that additional effort was required to make sense of the report. Interestingly, Donald had not realized that no directional cues had been provided the readers. He had carefully planned the arrangement and fully expected viewers to immediately recognize his intended pattern. He was pleasantly surprised by the aleatory responses.

On the other hand, we have chosen the display of this report as an explicit attempt to provide for the chance procedure. The reader is intentionally given permission to read in whatever way appears salient and to undermine the authority of the text as transparent purveyor of information and ideas. We ask you to consider the effect of this format upon your reading. You may experience some of the decision making which non-conventional forms demand of the reader. The activity of sense-making afforded by the lack of familiar anchors may even become a kind of aesthetic experience, an experience in

something and test it, or say something to get somebody going, and then have a—have you—have the teacher comment on it. I just have never been able to feel like that, the first time. Even in some of the other classes, I felt like philosophy, which I thought was open. But that's one of the things, and I felt better for the counseling, because I felt we needed to get the things out. And it's been like hanging there for a long time. I have this idea about some people in the class, but, you know, that they don't care as much about some of this as they say. But they expect because of what came out in DF's class about some comments about people running somebody else behind their back, running down—running them down. And I think if you feel comfortable enough with someone, you could—you have the resp...—the consideration for them to call them to their face, not talk behind their back. And I was brought into DF's class; and which DF, I think, was—she allowed us to have that time. She had a specific idea, and, but she yet allowed that, be —you know, SQ, she allowed SQ to talk about that. So I just thought it was—I—I—both, for both part times, all three times I gained a lot from that.

Donald: When—when—during that—those two classes, at

which form and content, signifier and signified become a powerful, synthetic, informative whole.

Forms of Data Display

This report concerns an on-going study of a pilot teacher preparation program at Arizona State University. This program is entitled "Teaching for a Diverse Future" (TDF) (funded by the U.S. West Foundation). The study follows seven students through their experiences with the program, and attempts to ascertain changes in attitudes within such an experience. The report presents parts of a conversation with five of the seven students about their program experiences. Four forms of data display are used to present these excerpts. These forms are: linear chronological, conversational analysis, musical score, and soliloquy.

Conversation analysis

This format (See Fig. 1) indicates information about the vocal production patterns in the conversational process. It makes the actions of the researcher quite evident as only the researcher could have produced such a format. This suggests an auteur orientation to the transcript.

one point you stood up, N1, and you said, um, "I had this idea that, um, maybe the thing to do is—for me to—if I want to hear someone speak, I should go over to them and invite them to speak." Um, was that testing?

N1: Yeah, it was testing, (B laughs lightly) because one of the ones when I did—I did a presentation, and I hate going in front of people and talking so much, because it's just their—I don't know, I don't know where it comes from. But I don't like—I feel—I don't feel comfortable talking in front of and try to—I was raised with the idea you don't show off to people and stuff. That's considered showing off, and I don't like to do that. But I figured—this one presentation I did, I went with a couple of other people. Well, all right, you know, and I have other people with me, so it's not so—it's not like I'm showing off, they're here, other people are with me, so they'll be—they'll be looking, and they'll be talk—everybody will be looking at them too. So it's not like I'm having, having to show off. So then, um, I felt, "Well, if that helped me maybe, maybe it might help these other people also," maybe another approach that you could use to get people to express themselves since they don't have—they can feel comfortable with us. But I don't know, it—it wasn't taken—I don't think it was

The conventions used in this portion of transcript are as follows. The up and down arrows (↑ ↓) precede a word which either has intonation going up or down. The equal sign (=) indicates that there is no break between speakers.

taken right away. It was taken as me trying to force somebody; that wasn't my intention.

T: But, N1, if you would have went and took somebody and brought them up front, that would have been obvious, because you would have gotten somebody that

---

B: It ↑ did for the ↑ community ↓ building, the ↑ silence ↓ part.=

Donald: =No, I didn't—I mean—I mean the issues of "Is it gendered?" or etc. No, ↓ there was a lot of silence in the room in that discussion,

           a <u>lot</u> of silence.=

B: =That's 'cause, it seemed like we were> waitn' for people to don't talk, to go up there< ((laughs)).=

F: =See, I think it's just the <u>opposite</u> of you, I've had—

N1:   [They need that.]

Donald: [And they knew that.]

F: I just thought, ↑ "well (0.6) he's not directin' this to <u>me</u>, 'cause ↑ I ↓ talk." So just kind of - =

B: That's what I figured too. ((laughs))

F: =But I didn't take it that I shouldn't talk in the future. I just - I said, "Well, we'll ↑ give ↓ them the ↑ chance. If they want to talk, fine. If they don't want to talk, well, I'll just keep talking." (2.45)

Tom: So, what is the relationship of all this to, you know, becoming a teacher?

Figure 1

The brackets ([ ]) are meant to show either simultaneity or overlap in speech. The numbers in parentheses show lag time in 1/10 of a second increments (.6). The doubled parentheses show sounds outside of speech or indicate transcriber notations about quality of speech. The dashes (—) indicate a hesitation. The more dashes, the more hesitation

doesn't talk. That might have been putting them more on the spot than—

N1: Yeah. But I—I don't know, I don't know what's wrong with putting somebody on the spot. I don't mind somebody putting me on the spot, just call me up there—

B: But it—it also, for those few voices that talk the most, it's not our problem that we're the ones

between sounds. Lastly, the change in line indicates the end of one vocalization and the beginning of another. These changes are not necessarily grammatical nor do they necessarily indicate a new thought.

Analytically, conversational analysis (CA) attempts to delineate how real settings work to accomplish meaning. A major focus is on how turns are taken (literally who speaks when) as knowledge streams out from the conversation. In such an approach conversation is seen as organized interaction in which neither tacit rules of conduct nor details of vocal production are ever "disorderly, accidental, or irrelevant" (Schiffrin, 1994, p.236). Who interrupts who and when, and the use of vocal intonation and the like are governed by cultural rules. People learn how to use their voices to contribute to a particular flow of conversation. All parties negotiate meaning. CA typically focuses upon adjacent pairs of conversational turn–taking to understand how knowledge is offered and confirmed, corrected, or extended. Analysts seek a "basic set of rules…governing turn construction,…allocation of a next turn ,…and…transfer

that talk the most. That's how I…after the two class discussions, I felt more frustrated, like, "Well, am I suppose to—to dominate the floor or—or to talk now? Or am I just suppose to suck it up and wait? Or write it in my journal later and hopefully one of the professors will respond to that question" (laughs), you know. And so when you brought up that, I thought, "Oh, great, now we have to go through this again." It was kind of like the absentee one, when I had first, you know—when you guys talked about the absence stuff again, I was taking notes from LT that day. And I wrote on the top of it, "Absént – discússion – a–gáin," you know, because I didn't think there was any purpose to it. But the control thing, it started out with the clique thing, and then it went to, "Who talks the most?" and that kind of stuff—and I just kind of thought at the end— "Okay, let's get on to something that's more important (laughs)."

Tom: What is the relationship of all of this to, you know, becoming a teacher? Are you making some connections between that and your future role as a teacher or not?

N2: Most definitely for me, at least. I think—I think I'm more— I'm more in your—your classes this semester than the other two in so much not academic–wise, but my own personal views, most

so as to minimize gap and overlap" in the course of conversation (Sacks, et al., in Schiffrin, 1994, p. 238). These rules, discovered inductively, reveal "how participants manage tasks of conversation" in a particular socio–cultural setting (Shiffrin, 1994, p.242).

Musical score

Erickson (1995) provided evidence of how a transcript might be understood as a musical score, noting how classroom talk is sung:

> Pitch and timing are important cues to the literal sense that is being made by grammar and vocabulary…In the utterance of classroom talk the significance of pitch cues and grammar cues for discourse organization…is implicit and culturally conventional.…the "melodic" contours of American classroom talk help us to understand its literal meaning, if we come from the same cultural speech community as the other speakers in the scene. (p. 28)

Erickson's transcript was itself fashioned into a musical score, complete with notes, rhythmic markings, measure bars, and rests. He made it clear that examining the rhythms, shifts

of the things I already—I was already in line with, but it just deepened and gave me some almost like background. Like when we worked on the issue of control, I knew that—that's how I wanted to eventually be or, you know, strive to be, but I didn't know how I was going to get there; or, you know, I didn't—I didn't plan on having a traditional control setup in a classroom, but I didn't know exactly, you know, well, "Wow, was it going to be chaos then or what? What is my view on control?"—you know. And what is—what are my personal ethics?—you know, and that class, made me look at them, which is, I felt was great.

T: Also, it—to help, to look at the kids that we'll have in our class, because—because I'm like—I talk sometimes, but not all that much; and like I said in the class that day, I think the things I have to say are the same things that the other people say, but some of them can say it more eloquently. Like TD, she talks beautiful. And for me to get up and try to muddle through what—what I'm trying to say, I'll just wait and let her (laughs)—because we usually, you know, think along the same lines, but she can do it so much nicer. What are those little children that are sitting there and not saying anything, why aren't they, you know, are they feeling the same way? Or are they just

(♩= 112)

B: It↑ did for the↑ community↓ buil ding, the↑ si lence↓ part.=

Donald: =No, I didn't___ I___ I mean___I mean the issues of

"Is it gen dered?" or etc. No,↑ there was a lot of si lence in the room in that dis cus sion,

a lot of si lence.=

B: *accel.*
=That's 'cause, it seemed like we were> waitin' for peo ple to don't talk, to go up there<(((laughs)).=

F: =See, I think it's just the op po site of you, I've had___

N1: [They need that.]

Donald: [And they knew that.]

F: I just thought,↑ "Well (0.6) he's not direc tin' this to me, 'cause↑ I↓ talk."

So I just kind of==

B: That's what I figured too ((laughs))

F: =But I didn't take it that I should n't talk in the future I just

Figure 2

in speed, rise and fall of sound, and connected, over-lapped or simultaneous speech can contribute to an understanding of the relationships among speakers/interviewees.

Let us revisit our own conversation analysis passage, now analyzing it in terms of its musical qualities.(See Fig. 2) First, we note a motive from dissonance to consonance. B and E appear to disagree with each other. B later reaches agreement with E when she says "I figured that too." Specifically, B's speed increases (the words between > < are like sixteenth notes leading into thirty-second notes) and a chorus of voices enters: F speaks, N1 answers B and Donald offers his com-

totally lost? And—and wonder if—if they do know the stuff and they're just, you know, just being shy and quiet or if they're just totally lost, or, you know.

F: If you write, if you write something out, most classes anyway—this class is a little different feeling but most classes. I feel if I can write it, at least I can erase my mistakes. Once I start speaking, it's said. Once it's said, you can—

N1: I don't know if—I don't know about—about eloquence, because the times I've heard T speak—speak, I—I was like impressed. The time you gave your report about the community, when you and DE, I enjoyed more what you had to say than what I—what I heard DE say, because it seemed like what you said was more concentrated and briefer —

ment *sotto voce*. This chorusing is a disjointed quartet recitative. The motive and recitative are resolved when F asserts that he was outside this expectation and B echoes this feeling. Rhythmically B began the episode by speaking more rapidly and was joined by a chorus of short, punctuated interjections resolving in the continuous flow between F and B. The episode ends in silence and a new phrase of conversational music is initiated by Tom Barone.

A musical rendering thus provides for several new possibilities. A straight chronological transcript tends to focus attention upon the individual and gives a sense of how one person's discourse can shift the conversation by contributing new topics or a new perspective. But the musical score version of the transcript displays the conversation in more simultaneity; it is closer to the actual experience of conversation. And when the transcript is seen as a musical score the collaboration to create meaning is more directly disclosed. The rhythms of speech let us see how people actually work together, looking for opportunities to intervene, add, or redirect. Speakers will often seek musical rests as openings and I just like the way you said it— I just, you know, T really, "Hey, come on talk more."

T: But see, there's a lot of stuff we didn't say...

N1: And times, but the times that you come out there, T, I've really been a lot more affected. I've been a lot more influenced by what you've said than some other people who talk a lot.

T: There's a lot more...

N1: Now, I want—you know, that eloquence, you have an eloquence.

T: There was more that should have been said that wasn't said, I just got in front of a crowd and went "Uh." You made more interviews than the one that I talked about.

N1: I enjoyed what you had to say. In fact, I even told F later, "God, I wish T would say more," because when she says something it's—it just got to me. I mean, it just made me think in a certain way different than the others, which is what the way you came out and said it in your report on the community, I just—I liked it.

T: It's a situation—I mean the—the setting because in my church group, you know, I'm the one that talks all the time (laughs), you know — and, um, but in the school, you know, it's just, I hold back a lot.

Tom: What's the difference there?

into which they may insert their discourse. When they desire to work out differences we can see them conspiring through the sounds they make. Conversation at cross-purposes tends to display rather different rhythmic and intonational activities and patterns. In these and other ways understanding the transcript as music opens up possibilities that other approaches to data analysis and display do not.

Soliloquy

Finally, there is soliloquy. In this mode we gather together the utterances of one member of the focus group as if there were no interlocutors present. These utterances are treated as if they had been presented in an uninterrupted, continuous fashion. In this form the *voice* of the individual sounds somewhat different from being presented as one voice among many others. One may think of the voice as that of a professor informing her students of some important information. The *voice*, speaking at some length, becomes authoritative.

In the academy this privilege is usually afforded to teachers, instructors, professors who aim to structure the knowledge of students, to pro-

T: I've just been there forever, and I just know—you know, I feel comfortable, I may know the people, and I just like—when you get into something.

Tom: You feel like they already know that you're not eloquent?

T: Yeah, they know me (laughs).

Tom: Is that it? —but that you have—

T: —and if I say something that—

Tom: —other people here haven't figured that out yet, and so you're reticent? Is that how you feel?

T: Because they—If I—If I say something that's off the wall, I'll know they'll either come back and ask me about it or they'll just blow it off.

Donald: They won't look at you strangely?

T: And they—but they're not going to give me a grade on it either, so . (laughs).

Tom: Um–hum.

B:That's funny, because at church I don't speak at all. I cannot stand up in front of the group unless—or I talk so fast, I like shoot off the podium (laughs). And if we're like in a women's retreat and they want us to stand up and say what we're thankful for, my pastor who is sitting next to me will say, "If you really want to stand up, I'll stand up with you," because I just go mute (laughs).

fess particular positions. But in soliloquy display the voice of the speaker is a student, whose voice seems extremely coherent and authoritative. Perhaps this wholeness and authority are dangerous illusions, for the circumstances of the discourse were fragmented and interventions and contradictions did occur. In reality this speaker was one among many.

But the illusion of a unified, singular voice, preserves an important aspect of human consciousness: an individual rarely feels disjunctures of character or role as she moves through her day. Whether in the classroom or on the bus, eating lunch or preparing for bed, her sense of self is rather continuous. Even if the pulls of various daily events make her feel torn apart by the demands of life, she still feels a sense of selfhood. While postmodernists have come to understand that the self is really a bundle of selves socially constituted and organized via power relationships, our daily experience is of the integrity of self. Fragmenting individual speech in transcript display yields certain kinds of information but hides this sense of personal coherence. Graphically displaying a person's utter-

Donald: Now, now, why is that?

B: I don't know. I just get so nervous. And then, you know, I sit down, and I'm just like this. I am just, just totally, totally different. I guess here I feel more freer—I know I'm talking I'm making sense. There, I know that I couldn't mess up at that church (laughs), but, uh, I don't know. Because I get off the podium, and I'm just near tears, just "uhhh" (laughs), you know. I'm so glad I don't have to go back up there. And during prayer service or something on a Wednesday night if I do go, I want to say something. And I usually just say it quietly to myself, but I don't stand...

Tom:...your set of beliefs, and, in fact, that the beliefs, uh, that sort—sort of at the center of the TDF Program, right, and that there's some people who might feel that they are not quite in line with that set of beliefs. Yeah, could you all talk about that—in terms of your own, um, feelings, if—in speaking—with—with the assurance that you're not being evaluated.

N2: Um, I know for myself right away with—starting with Tom and DG's class, and Tom was very ambiguous where he was going, and for some reason I saw it after the first day of class exactly where he was going. And everyone was griping and moaning. I didn't really know anyone, so I didn't say

ances together in one space underscores the sense of wholeness. Notice:

"I talk sometimes, but not all that much; and like I said in the class that day, I think the things I have to say are the same things that the other people say, but some of them can say it more eloquently. Like TD, she talks beautiful. And for me to get up and try to muddle through what—what I'm trying to say, I'll just wait and let her (laughs)—because we usually, you know, think along the same lines, but she can do it so much nicer. What are those little children that are sitting there and not saying anything, why aren't they, you know, are they feeling the same way? or are they just totally lost?…And—and wonder if—if they do know the stuff and they're just, you know, just being shy and quiet or if they're just totally lost, or, you know. And it's a situation—I mean the—the setting because in my church group, you know, I'm the one that talks all the time (laughs), you know—and, um, but in the school, you know, it's just, I hold back a lot….I've just been there forever, and I just know—you know, I feel comfortable, I may know the peo-

anything, cause, I didn't see any reason to. And, uh, but, yeah, I—I noticed right away again I saw the hidden agenda almost, you know—there is almost one, you know, you guys, would hopefully like to have an end product of, you know, 33 whole language teachers. And maybe they're Republicans, maybe their Democrats; that's not the point (laughs)…as far as I can see.

F: Myself, I had no idea—well, when I got into—When I decided to try to become a teacher, I—I really was confused as to really what I wanted to do. I didn't think that one person could really make that much difference in a classroom, but I wanted to do something different than the way I was taught when I was younger—I knew that was not the way I wanted to do it—when I got into the TDF Program, because I was listening to Tom and DG and DF, and Don and NF, TI, I started thinking, "Well, you know, this control business"—because I would have been a control teacher. I can—I know I would have been a really, "Hey, I am in front. It's my classroom. You do as I tell you, and we'll get this done." And after taking the class, I realized that that was totally wrong. It's a—the control should be in the children's hands more. I'm just there to guide them and help them along. And—and I've—I've

ple, and I just like—when you get into something... If I say something that's off the wall, I'll know they'll either come back and ask me about it or they'll just blow it off...but they're not going to give me a grade on it either, so. I think that there's a, a, um,...that you know, we all know what the TDF is about, but I think, um, when we went into it I think a lot of us thought that it was our opinions were going to be, um, matter more than they do; because in that ethics paper I wrote, everything that was underlined in red was taken right out of the book. Anything that was put in that was mine (laughs) wasn't addressed. So, you know, there's—you—the things that you want to come out of the prog—you know, you still have the—you still have the hidden agenda—the—the things that you want us to understand that you ... And, um, it was—as far as DE and the Democrat-Republican thing, in my paper I put, there was one comment that said, "We're one nation under God," and I put down that if—if we're one nation under God, we'll do this and we'll—you know. And—and everytime I did that, you put—everytime I said "He," thinking, you know, addressing God, you put, you

tried it with my own children, uh, not to a lot of degree. I feel I have some kind of vision, but I have bent a lot. And—and it makes a difference. It does work more than saying, "Hey, this is what has to be done." If you can get them to say, "This is what I want to do," it works a lot better. They enjoy it, they do—they do a better job. It's just that, uh, children have to have the responsibility of learning back in their hands – you have to make it enjoyable and meaningful for them or it just won't happen, that's the way I look at it.

(Pause)

N1: As far as the TDF Program, thank God for it, thank Hu–Sen for it – I mean as far, uhhh, I was like frustrated for a long time in school, but I maintained, because I take a stoic—I didn't know there was such a thing as stoicism until I got to school. But it's—it's throughout—it's similar to philosophy, western philosophy. Marcus Aurelius is one of the ones that I really like reading about. And, uh, then it kind of goes along the lines with the way I was brought up, because I was brought up that you take things—no matter hard they are, you just take them into stride and hope things will be better. That's in our history, I mean all through it, you know, as I was underlined that in red and said, at the end you said, um, what about those people that think He is a She or that think He is more than One. I think there's no, you know, there's no—how you address them? And I just thought, "Well, he's wrong" (laughs). But I know where you stand (laughs). (Laughter) But, um, but I've gotten into this program that—that a lot of my ideas have changed, and I've worked with kids for almost 20 years now and—in the traditional setting —and the one class I liked the most was more of an open— you know, the—the kids could talk, and I liked that a lot more —and I think that's like this program. I'm going hold on to a lot my ideas, but a lot of them have been changed. And I've even put a lot of them in practice with the kids I work with now, second, third, and fourth graders in Sunday School. And I don't have them just sitting at the desks doing the worksheets (laughs). I mean it's so bad now that they've moved us in this room that have sliding doors where the adults are outside in—in the next room. Every Sunday they come in and they go "Shhh," because I let the kids do, and they were getting excited one time, "Look what I

growing up, and I used to hear my mom and my grandpa talk and my dad, that's the way it is – you just have to work with it.

Tom: Are you referring to yourself as a Native American then?

N1: Yeah, yeah. And so that's how you weather it—the—the main thing is to get through and help your children to get through. And then maybe you can make a difference.

T: I think that there's a, a, um,...that you know, we all know what the TDF is about, but I think, um, when we went into it I think a lot of us thought that it was our opinions were going to be, um, matter more than they do; because in that ethics paper I wrote, everything that was underlined in red was taken right out of the book. Anything that was put in that was mine (laughs) wasn't addressed. So, you know, there's—you—the things that you want to come out of the prog—you know, you still have the—you still have the hidden agenda—the—the things that you want us to understand that you want us to know.

Tom: Don't you sometimes feel irritated though at the times when you feel your beliefs are not being validated?

T: Not irritated if they can support what they're trying—how they're trying to change my mind, if I can see what they're trying to do. Otherwise, my beliefs, the things

got. Look what I made." And, you know, they were excited about what they were doing; and I thought they were getting more out of it than they would if—if you were just sitting at the table reading the story – and I don't sit and read the story anymore (laughs), so I've learned in DF's and NF's classes of other ways to do it. And that's the same thing, I think, comparing that to—to the program, there's a lot of things I'm going to hold on to, but there's a lot of things that have changed my ideals about teaching—you know, it's not going to be…the thing that's most important to me, that's what we were doing. We were all in a group, and they had that—their ceremony was we took talking sticks and they went around, and everybody said what was most important to them. And I said, "My beliefs"—something like that, "My beliefs and my two daughters are the most important thing to me." A lot of other people were able to say, you know, their religion, or their daughter, whatever was the most important to them, and a lot of people didn't. A lot of people said their husband, their boyfriend, you know, whatever it was. But we felt free enough that we talked

that I really hold dear to me are so grounded that, um, unless they can really show me, you know, to try to sway me one way or the other, I'll listen. But, you know, there's got to be a lot of proof.

Donald: Did you take it that I was telling you you were wrong when I asked you to consider others who would want to refer to God as She?

T: No, because at the end of it, after you said, what about, what about, you said, "How would you address these people?"

B: Yeah, I think our diversity is valued in TDF, the whole point of it, but each one of us are going to be teachers, but we're all going to be different. I mean I'd really like to see what our classrooms turn out to be in five years after we've had some experience and be able to put some of this stuff in—in what DF's saying and what—how we do our community and how we do our literature and all these things, and how we would make it work in our class. I know I kind of keep school, education separate from my political beliefs, because I don't really see them—you know, I see them corresponding somewhat theoretically. But personally, I'm Republican, and I vote certain ways for other reasons other than school. And most of TDF, I think the majority of you, would not agree with most—most of the reasons why I vote, but those are

about it and not—I mean he could have—in the paper, he could have just, you know, not mentioned it at all, but I thought that was kind of cute (laughs) that was—you know, that he addressed it. When he does bring up his Jewish religion, it's to make a point to help us understand some other concept. It's not just to tell us about—I was uncomfortable when I went up in the middle to say what I said. (laughs)....Yeah, when I said, I—something about, um, some of us might not have something to say; or we wanted to listen to the other people to see if we're on track, just, you know, just—or they can say the stuff better than—or, you know, you know, choose better words than— And it was— I was uncomfortable because you know everybody's listening to you and you want to get your point across – and sometimes you—you just can't find the words to say it. I was uncomfortable....But, Donald, you know what, because it was all—the conversation was suppose to be on, on um, those two classes, a lot of the people that don't talk up in that classes were in those small groups. Almost everybody has them, in all the three different classes."

my personal—these are what I do with my family, with my friends that make who I am; and the teaching part is going to be all part of that person, me. And the stuff I'm learning in DF's class and the community aspects in Donald's and, you know, the different models of education in yours, all those things I'm picking up pieces of it. And, you know, it will fall into place. And I'm not really worried about it. Yeah, my views on education have changed. Like you said, we're persuaded to think—we're being persuaded to come out of TDF as certain types of teachers. And I think that you're doing a good job with that, because when I read the articles, to me now it makes sense. And so I think we are being persuaded this way, which I think is great, because that's what people are being persuaded in the other programs in their ways. Because my—my brother-in-law is—I told him we had to do the bibliography in Maryann's class. He's like, "That is so bunch a, bunch a crap," and da, da, da, da – and I just looked at him like, "Don't you want your kids to read?" –you know– "Don't you think you should—" and I start talking to him, and he's just a blank wall. I mean it's like talking to cement. And I was just like, "This is incredible," you know. Donald: So let's—let's try to stick this—this question, when did you

References

Barone, T. (1978). *Inquiry into classroom experiences: A qualitative holistic approach.* Unpublished doctoral dissertation, Stanford University, Stanford, CA.

Barone, T. & Eisner, E. (in press). Arts–based educational research. In R. Jaeger (Ed.), *Complementary Methods for Research in Education,* (2nd ed.), Washington, D.C.: American Educational Research Association.

Blumenfeld–Jones, D. (1993, April). *Teacher's ideas about pleasure and learning: Critical interviews.* Paper presented at the meeting of the American Educational Research Association, Atlanta, GA.

Blumenfeld–Jones, D.S., Donmoyer, R., Yennie–Donmoyer, J., Gabella, M., Kinzer, C., Flinders, D., Rossman, G., & Reynolds, A. (1995, April). *Modes of presentation: A discussion about three alternative forms.* Paper presented at the meeting of the American Educational Research Association, San Francisco, CA.

Bresler, L. (1995). A symposium on arts, knowledge, and education. *Educational Theory, 45* (1),1–84.

Buber M. (1970). *I and Thou.* (W. Kauffman, Trans.). New York: Charles Scribner's Sons.

Donmoyer, R. (1989, October). *Readers' theater as pedagogical method.* Presented at the Conference on Curriculum Theory and Classroom Practice, Dayton, OH.

Donmoyer, R. (1994, April). *In their own words: A readers theater presentation of students' writing about writing and a discussion of the pros and cons of artistic modes of data display.* Paper presented at the meeting of the American Educational Research Association, New Orleans, LA.

Eisner, E. (1975). Educational connoisseurship and educational criticism: Their forms and functions in educational evaluation. *Journal of Aesthetic Education*, Bicentennial Issue.

Eisner, E. (1977). On the use of educational connoisseurship and educational criticism for the evaluation of classroom life. *Teachers College Record, 78* (3), 325–388.

Erickson, R. (1995). The music goes round and round: How music means in schools. *Educational Theory, 45* (1), 19–34.

Fish, S. (1980). *Is there a text in this class? The authority of interpretive communities.* Cambridge, MA: Harvard University Press.

Jeffers, C.S. (1993). Research as art and art as research: A living relationship. *Art Education, The Journal of the National Art Education Association, 46* (5), 12–17.

Kristeva, J. (1986). Stabat mater. In T. Moi (Ed.), *The Kristeva reader.* (pp. 160-186) New York: Columbia University Press.

McCutcheon, G. (1976). *The disclosure of classroom life.* Unpublished doctoral dissertation, Stanford University, Stanford, CA.

Richards, M.C. (1962). *Centering in pottery, poetry, and the person.* Middletown, CT: Wesleyan University Press.

Robbe-Grillet, A. (1957). *La jalousie.* Paris: Editions de Minuit.

Schiffrin, D. (1994). *Approaches to discourse.* England and Cambridge, MA: Blackwell.

Sears, J. (1989, October). *"Prisms" play/workshop.* Paper presented at the Conference on Curriculum Theory and Classroom Practice, Dayton, OH.

Trousdale, A., Adams, N., Jacobs, M. E., Munro, P., & Quinn, M. (1994, April). *Womentalkin': A reader's theater performance of teachers' stories.* Paper presented at the meeting of the American

Educational Research Association, New Orleans, LA.

Vallance, E. (1975). *Aesthetic criticism and curricular description*. Unpublished doctoral dissertation, Stanford University, Stanford, CA.

CHAPTER SIX

JANICE JIPSON
NICHOLAS PALEY

CURRICULUM AND ITS UNCONSCIOUS

The rigor of proportion,
the revolt of art, and the jolting happiness
of Take it or Leave it (seriously).

How can we acknowledge the gifts
our doubts give us?

How will you become
the change you want (to make)
in the world?

What is not apparent
to the dreaming mind
is unavailable
to the daring eye.

When we hold our imagination to
our ear, what do we hear?
Is it the ocean?
Is it a roar?
Is it a habit for devotion
that we have never heard before?

As questions become more and more
specialized and emphasis is increasingly
placed on the histories of material things,
what, if any, will be
the role of poetry and the energies of
subversive understanding?

Conflict and the recognitions
produced by statements removed
from calculation, detached from
method—irregular, jagged,
inconsistent.

It is denial,
not devotion, desire, despair.

Can one imagine a critique
that would not be customary,
that would not be categorical,
but through (by?) which
issues of custom and category
would be engaged?

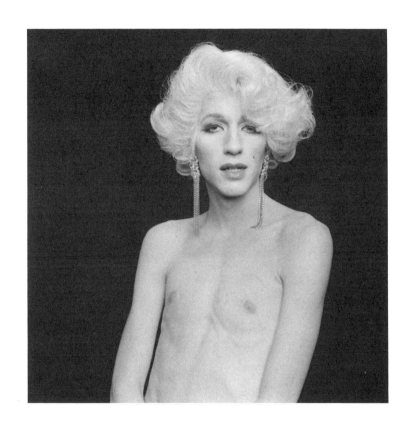

Does a language, a thinking
of elasticity, of insistence
only develop when it struggles
to escape the shadow of
another?

We want to create feeling,
but not in the literal sense
of making it emerge from
the usual romance (echo effect).

To explore activities removed
from any externally constructed
narrative: What's coherence
got to do with it?

Visual Documentation

(in order of image appearance)

Marc Chagall, *The Angel and the Reader*, c. 1930. Gouache on wove paper.

Peter Blume, *The Rock*, 1948. Oil on canvas.

Martin Johnson Heade, *Magnolias*, 1886-1890. Oil on canvas.

Jeanne Dunning, *Neck*, 1990. Photograph.

Edgar Degas, *The Bathers*, 1895-1905. Pastel and charcoal on tracing paper, pierced and mounted on board.

Arthur Dove, *Silver Sun*, 1929. Oil and metallic paint on canvas.

John Frederick Kensett, *Coast at Newport*, 1869. Oil on canvas.

William Bradford, *The Coast of Labrador*, 1866. Oil on canvas.

Annie Adjchavanich, *David to Marilyn*, 1993. Photograph.

Bartolomeo Manfredi, *Cupid Chastised*, c. 1605/1610. Oil on canvas.

Ferdinand Hodler, *The Grand Muveran*, 1912. Oil on canvas.

Cy Twombly, *August Notes from Rome (Ferragosto)*, 1961. Oil, oil crayon, and pencil on canvas.

All images courtesy of the Art Institute of Chicago, except for Jeanne Dunning, *Neck*, courtesy of the artist; Annie Adjchavanich, *David to Marilyn*, courtesy of Hemphill Fine Arts; and Cy Twombly, *August Notes from Rome (Ferragosto)*, courtesy of the Hirshhorn Museum and Sculpture Garden, Smithsonian Institution, Gift of Joseph H. Hirshhorn, 1966 (Photo: Lee Stalsworth).

A PLACE FROM WHICH TO SPEAK
STORIES OF MEMORY, CRISIS AND STRUGGLE FROM THE PRESCHOOL CLASSROOM

Prologue: A Story of Theory

I begin this essay with many questions about the possibilities of telling the stories of one's life. We all carry with us in our bodies, minds and hearts the memories of those moments in our lives which changed us forever. We have been changed by force, by effort, by the promise of something more than we already had. As I write this chapter, this paragraph, this word, I awake those sore, callous, and even pleasurable places in which the joyous, painful, and ordinary memories of my life as a preschool teacher, as an activist, as an artist, as an academic lie and wait for me to remember. I have chosen in this essay to return to what could be considered very ordinary memories of my teaching. In choosing to re-remember everyday stories of my teaching, I hope to locate the extraordinary within them. This writing is an attempt to seek out the possibilities of transformation and change in the everyday experiences that subtly shift our consciousnesses and our bodies. In re-remembering and retelling, I re-create the possibility for change in my beliefs about children, my beliefs about what it means to be a teacher and my concrete teaching practices.

The retelling of the stories of my teaching in the context of this (academic) chapter exceeds simply changes to my own psyche and teaching practices: it changes the theory and history of academic practice in early childhood education. To draw on the power of personal stories in an academic context is to confront and intersect with the stories created theoretically and historically about teachers and children. History, theory and research are in themselves stories which shape our experience and the ways in which we remember and retell. Research is and always has been a way to tell stories of experience, and similarly, the history and theory we create shapes the ways in which both old and new stories are told.

I do not want to argue about the nature of (T)ruth or the existence of the (R)eal and the ways that theory and research are used in that struggle. I do, however, want to acknowledge that such a struggle exists and recognize, if not use, this tension between the real and the fictive in my use of research and theory. It must be recognized that I cannot retell stories of my teaching without retelling and rewriting theory as well. Additionally, the history of women telling stories of their teaching creates a location from which I am invited to speak. These histories and theories are as much my stories as the retelling of my experiences as a teacher. In this essay, events, theory, research and history merge to create a testimony to the struggle I face in the attempt to rethink my life as a teacher of young children.

I do not come to this moment alone, however. Many women stand and speak beside me as I wade through and attempt to write through my memories of teaching, as those memories merge with research and theory. There is a long history of resistance to the silence surrounding women's experience, resistance mounted through stories.

Hearing What Has Been Hidden:
Feminism and the Struggle for Voice

Feminist methodologies have marked a place where

personal truths and subjective experience have become a powerful location of political and social change in the concrete lives of women. At its most powerful, narrative work has the potential to move one from silence to speech, and, as hooks (1989) suggests, "moving from silence to speech is for the oppressed, the colonized, the exploited, and those who stand and struggle side by side a gesture of defiance that heals, that makes new life and new growth possible. It is the act of speech, of 'talking back,' that is no mere gesture of empty words, that is the expression of our movement from object to subject-the liberated voice" (p.9). This movement from object to subject is precisely what the biographers of teachers' lives have done in their work.

Within educational research there has been a growing amount of work that makes central the stories told in and about classrooms. Like the research generated out of feminist oriented studies, the work of many educational biographers and narrative inquirers concerns itself with examining and facilitating change within the oppressive modes of the classroom. The effect of this concern for actual life experiences of teachers and children has brought about several important traditions within the field, based on self-disclosure and testimony.

Within teacher research, there has been an increasingly strong orientation toward teachers researching themselves and their classrooms. This work shares both feminist and anthropological/ethnographic origins. Elizabeth Cochran-Smith (1992), Sue Middleton (1987), Madeline Grumet (1988), and Janet Miller (1992) have produced extensive work which explicitly seeks to listen to and convey women's experiences as educators as they speak for themselves. Further, this work is part of a larger reflection on how educational locations (curriculum, in particular) are generated out of these experiences. Janet Miller (1992) explains the importance of autobiographical work in educational research: "(a)utobiographical work attempts to acknowledge, and to examine as knowledge, the interwoven relationships among one's educational experience, one's contextualizations of that experience with social-political worlds, and one's constructions of curriculum as both reflecting and creating those worlds" (p. 113).

The foregrounding of teachers' voices is primary to this work. Often included in these texts are indexical autobiographical sections revealing personal information about the author/investigator as well. This practice has meant an important move away from the invisible inquirer. We can no longer ignore the workings of these gendered systems as radical investigative work has called into question the notion of objective research and directly implicated the researcher in the outcome of the investigation. The autobiographical notes are an attempt to make available the biases of personal experience (of the researcher). The import of these biographers, biases and all, is to listen to and record the stories of teaching, the stories of "I."

Listening to Ourselves: Stories of "I"

Some researcher/teachers have taken a more personal focus and made the story of their investigation/teaching central rather than indexical. Sue Middleton (1987) uses her own childhood paintings to explore the development of her relationship to the Maori people and imperialism during the process of her schooling as a child of European descent in New Zealand. This work is powerful as she juxtaposes her voice as a child artist and as an adult academic, revealing depth and subtlety in the formation of racial and cultural knowledge.

Naomi Norquay (1991), as well, uses her own childhood experiences to explore her adult understandings and reactions to racial dynamics. Norquay has done extensive memory work in order to "re-member" and rethink her early experiences as a "white" child in classrooms with Afro-Canadian children. This work has helped her to bring into her critical consciousness those experiences and ideas about race which influence her work as a researcher, a teacher, a human being.

Although Norquay's work is unique in its use of memory, there is a considerable tradition of teachers reflecting on the significance of race and other issues of social justice in their classrooms and in their lives. In the work of both Sylvia Ashton-Warner (1963, 1967) and Vivian Gussin Paley (1979, 1992) *the stories they tell are their teaching*. One cannot be separated from the other in that they come to understand themselves and their students through a curriculum based on self-reflectivity and storytelling. Sylvia Ashton-Warner's teaching and writing was part of a life-long process of self-reflection and transformation. Throughout her teaching in New Zealand in the 1930's, 40's, 50's, and 60's, she kept journals about her experiences working with Maori children as well as with children of European descent. Later, she turned these personal accounts into both fiction and nonfiction books. This work provocatively calls into question the role of women, the impact of race, and the possibility of change in classrooms and in the way people live. In using her own experiences as a teacher as the text of her writing, she has located her own learning in this process of self-reflection and testimony. In doing so, she recognizes the possibilities of change in this recording and telling of the story of the classroom.

Vivian Gussin Paley also understands this power. She has transformed the curriculum of the classroom itself into a locus of storytelling. The children of her preschool classroom spend their time generating, writing and acting out the stories which make up their lives. Vivian Gussin Paley has learned the value of this curriculum through her own work as a writer and storyteller. Like Sylvia Ashton-Warner, she records her days as a teacher in a personal journal. She also tape records the events of her classroom and spends her evenings going back over the happenings of the day. Out of these "data," she has written the books which document her transformation as a teacher and as a person. The books are as much about the children in her classrooms as they are about her, because, as she articulates so well through her stories, it is the interactions, the moments of being a teacher, which challenge and change the way she teaches.

The significance of these women's writings lies in its reiteration that transformation is the crucial moment of teaching, and it is through the stories we(I) tell about our(my) teaching that we(I) may enter and work within that moment, transforming ourselves(myself) and the possibilities of the next moment. Herein lies both the promise and the challenge of my teaching and of this writing.

A Place From Which to Speak: The Story of the Stories

> ...resistance is also a 'struggle against forgetting.' Remembering makes us subjects in history. It is dangerous to forget. (Felman & Laub, 1992, p. 96)

One has many stories which one can and must tell. These stories are sorted out of recollection and memory, prompted by questions, the rereading of journal entries, listening to audio recordings, and viewing photographs and video tapes. One must sort through the variety of images and emotion each memory/story might invoke. One may never fully "remember" the events of a moment (even as a video tape might play back the event minute by minute). Memories are not as available to us as we might like; they cannot be easily retrieved and examined. Our memories lie interwoven between text and dream, between desire and fear, among wishes, hopes, and disappointments. Remembering and telling can be an arduous moment, a conflation between truth and lies, between past and present, between remembering and forgetting. We must navigate the complexities of memory in order to tell stories which are meaningful to us and others. The struggle in remembering, then, is to reconstruct the stories in which we find our "truths."

> Testimony cannot be authentic without…crisis, which has to break and to transvaluate previous categories and previous frames of reference. (Felman & Laub, 1992, p. 54)

Given the complexity of memory, I cannot tell you the "true" story or even the most "important" story of my teaching. I have chosen then to reconstruct those moments which have left me with uncertainty and doubt. These are the times in my work with children where thought and action intersect in such a way that the roles and rules of our classroom break down. At these moments, what I thought to be true about teaching and children collapses; what I know about the world cannot account for what I have seen; what I know about myself makes it impossible for me to react. These are memories of fear and desire, a longing for certainty. It is a chronicle of moments of ordinary crisis in my life as a teacher. It is a witnessing of both my "failure to imagine" (Felman & Laub, 1992, p. 105) children and my teaching differently and, at times, my ability to move successfully within uncertain frames of reference, becoming a subject to the history which is unfolding. This is the documentation of my "encounters with the real" (Felman & Laub, 1992, p. 167) in my teaching, the possibilities and failures to transform.

As I struggle to construct this story for you now, I am struck by the lack of words available to describe my experiences as a teacher, as a writer, as a storyteller. I am, in many ways, a storyteller caught in a crisis of language. I push and play with the meanings of words in order to convey the complicated and sometimes contradictory understandings I have of my experiences in the classroom and as an academic. I have drawn on the voices of other feminist storytellers to create a place from which I can speak. Their words foreshadow and support the stories I create here. Theory also helps support the stories that I create by deconstructing and reconstructing meaning and under-standing. Theory can make words mobile and transitory. Theory can open up places for stories to be told that did not previously exist. As I move into my own recollections about my preschool teaching, I want to contextualize my memories in relation to the theories which shape my retellings.

The Theories

> Theory as non-theory leaves the field open. For, it is in the space of such voiding that theory can be said to come closest to poetry, making possible analytical discourses that take into account crises of meaning, subject, and structure.... (Trinh, 1989a, p. 5)

Discourse

> ...all manifest discourse is secretly based on an 'already-said'; that this 'already-said' is not merely a phrase that has already been spoken, or a text that has already been written, but a 'never-said', an incorporeal discourse, a voice as silent as a breath, a writing that is merely the hollow of its own mark. (Foucault, 1972, p. 25)

Discourse is that which speaks to us orally or textually about both the internal and social rules of our existence. It is the moment between the law and the body. In *Teaching the Postmodern*, Brenda Marshall (1992) draws on Foucault to describe discourse as that which "refers to a regulated system of statements which can be analyzed not solely in terms of its internal rules of formation, but also as a set of practices within a social milieu. Discourse is the combina-tion of a practice and a mode or structure of speaking" (p. 99). I employ this notion of discourse here in order to rethink the internal and social formation of the body of the teacher (my teacher body). In other words, I am concerned with the ways in which social, political and cultural notions of "teacher" (the "already-said") work silently (as silent as a breath) to construct the internal rules of formation as well as the social practices of my work with children.

Text

> The Text is in motion: it is 'a process of demonstration,' 'exists in the movement of a discourse,' is 'experienced only in an activity of production.' (Marshall, 1992, p. 123)

An important part of this story is my effort to rethink the texts which are constituted by and constituting of the events of our lives. It is through these texts that discourses are written on our bodies, minds and souls. In each moment we act within the immediacy of the event, our responses performing these complicated texts within the discourses which both create and contradict them. These are tightly woven constructions of the self located in relation to and constituted by the discourses which have made one's life. I am not, however, referring to an essentialized identity located within the consciousness or unconsciousness of the subject. *Self-texts* are constituted out of the moment of discursive practice, within the event itself in an activity of production. They are the internalization and performance of discourse.

In my work with children I perform particular *self-texts* which constitute "teaching." These *self-texts* are constructed by the discourses of early education and developmental psychology as I have come to embody them. Also at work in my performance as teacher are those *self-texts* generated out of the discourses that construct common sense knowledge of adults and children in general. The texts multiply as one considers the ways that knowledge has been constructed in relation to gender, race, class, ability, and sexual preference. No *self-text* operates definitively, however. Each is constantly in the process of being challenged and rewritten by conflictual discursive and non-discursive texts.

Performance

> Such acts, gestures, enactments...are performative in the sense
> that the essence or identity that they otherwise purport to
> express are fabrications manufactured and sustained through
> corporeal signs and other discursive means. (Butler, 1990, p. 136)

Judith Butler (1990), in her work on gender and sexuality, has proposed an image of self which locates the gendered, sexual self not in the internal essentialized subject, but in the performative "acts, gestures, and enactments" (Butler, 1990, p. 136) of discursive practice. These performative acts both create and legitimize the discourses which surround identity and behavior, seeking to eliminate all that would contradict the coherence of the text. Judith Butler (1990) explains: "...identification (is) an enacted fantasy or incorporation...it is clear that coherence is desired, wished for, idealized, and that this idealization is an effort of a corporeal signification" (p. 136). Through the performative body one attempts to signify the coherency of identity. In addition, it is the desire for this coherency that drives the performance. I suggest that teaching is equally performative, borne out of desire for coherency in the self-text of "teacher", which is constituted by the discourse in the field of early childhood education. Other self-texts play out similarly, seeking through performance, the affirmation of their reality. The interactions within the classroom are played out among the corporeal performances of "teacher," "student," "adult," "child," "white," "black," and whatever other "identities" the children and I bring with us. My stories represent a blending and clashing of these performative texts in the moment of teaching.

Excess

> Representation follows two laws: it always conveys more than
> it intends; and it is never totalizing. The 'excess' meaning conveyed by representation creates a supplement that makes mul-

tiple and resistant readings possible. (Phelan, 1993, p. 2)

Performance, however, can never contain that which it seeks to represent. In terms of gender, the performance of "femaleness" can never fully represent the experience of being female: "female" as lived experience always exceeds the bounds of corporeal or discursive representation. Likewise, "teacher," "adult," "child" are, as these experiences are lived, beyond what can be expressed through the performative boundaries of the self-texts which attempt to contain them. This moment of "excess," is for Judith Butler, one of psychic excess: it is that which cannot be accounted for in ontological constructions which locate identity and "choice" within the "volitional subject" (1990, p. 137). My retellings then, are an attempt to look precisely at *that which cannot be accounted for*, the crisis in representation and the "failure to imagine" (Felman & Laub, 1992, p. 105) that which cannot be contained by the bounds of the self-text. It is with great effort that I push through the cracks of my own crystallized self-text to read the nontextual, the psychic texts of crisis as expressed in power, desire, and voice.

The Stories

> Something must be said. Must be said that has not been *and* has been said before. 'It will take a long time, but the story must be told. There must not be any lies' (Leslie Marmon Silko). It will take a long time for living cannot be told, not merely told: living is not livable. Understanding, however, is creating, and living, such a immense gift that thousands of people benefit from each past or present life being lived. The story depends upon every one of us to come into being. It needs us all, needs our remembering, understanding, and creating what we have heard together to keep on coming into being. (Trinh, 1989b, p. 119)

I turn now to my own retellings, and the importance of sharing them here. In this portion of my story, I am both the witness to children's stories, the biographer of their experience, and I am the witness to my own experience, the autobiographer. I understand these teaching experiences in complicated ways: emotion, intellect, and physical sensation intertwine and collide. How I convey this understanding in my writing becomes a crucial methodological point.

The stories I offer you in this section are not examples or facts. They are the re-creation of moments of teaching remembered through my journals and audio tapes. They are vignettes, representations of ideas generated through my writing. They are tableaus whose meanings are specific to this work, this essay, this moment. The three stories I tell are not meant to illustrate any generalized notions about children, teaching or education. I do not propose to rewrite early childhood education or develop an alternative curriculum, per se. Neither do I intend to recount a moment of *personal* satisfaction, crisis or revelation. As I have explained earlier, these are *ordinary* moments. I am not specifically interested in "what I have learned" from these experiences. I have struggled to create here, a moment, temporarily possible only in the context of my larger story, in which I may return to the experience of my teaching. This is not an attempt to locate the personal or the universal, but to testify to the discourses which work through the lives of teachers and young children, to make myself subject to a history which is not and cannot be accounted for in empirical research. I have attempted to privilege neither the phenomenological nor the empirical, but rather, to locate the import of this work in the event and its intersection with radical theories of survival.

I recount three events, ordinary moments of crisis in meaning, moments which I could easily let slip away. In them, I explore elements which I recognize as functioning within and through discourse: voice, desire, and power. Each element functions simultaneously and in varying degrees to influence the ways in which discourse is acted upon and through individuals. These three vignettes recount the intersection of discourse, affect and action and the moment in which available meanings fail to contain them.

Power

A four year old child sits with two other children and two adults at a snack table. I make a request of him, to pass the crackers, to pick up his napkin, to stay seated while he is eating, each request referring to how I think snack should proceed. He stares deeply into my eyes and crushes his cracker in his hand and lets the pieces fall on the floor. I feel my chest fill. My heart beats more quickly. I have just been blatantly defied and challenged, and it makes me angry. I begin to think, "this is the first day I have ever met this child and he has just declared war against me. What the hell am I going to do?" His sister and his cousin sit watching. My thoughts continue, "I have spent the entire morning being nice to this child, and he is being a real jerk." I am hurt. My authority has been threatened, threatened by the will and glance of this child. This feeling of being threatened is not altogether different from fear.

Yet, I know that for children to push the boundaries of acceptable behavior with new adults is common. I suppress my hurt feelings, redirect my anger to "teacherly thoughts." I remember other situations which I have been in before. I remember early childhood theory about "testing." I put to use my "knowledge" of children, redirecting and making firm suggestions in order to help the child "set boundaries" for himself. There is still doubt, however, about the outcome of this situation. It is clear that he wants to challenge those boundaries. I feel compelled to establish that I am indeed "in charge."

I know on one level that this is impossible because he has, with the glance and a squeeze, engaged with "the pleasure of the text" of power (Barthes, 1975, p. 19). I know that the *jouissance* (p. 19) of rejecting the text is compelling, as I am often caught up in rejecting the texts through which power works on me. I understand that through this act this child is distinguishing himself from the text of the classroom and his role as student. In response, I am even more compelled to establish the coherence of my control, the text of "teacherness." An intense desire for coherence wells from deep inside me: for in challenging the text of the classroom, he has also created in me a crisis of self-text as teacher. Fear lies in the knowledge that the coherence of "classroom" (as it has been constructed by me via the discourse of early childhood education) is dependent upon the performance of fairly specific texts: my control, his capitulation. If the "classroom," as defined by unequal power relations, ceases to exist as text, then so do I as "teacher" in this context.

I ignore that other possibilities may lie in the breakdown of this oppressive text, hoping to re-establish the "balance" of control. This child's insubordination, however, is absolutely key to the workings of power in the class. The child must be free to choose to engage in the text of the classroom. If he is not free to make this choice, then his participation has been coerced, violent. A relationship of power is contingent upon the freedom to reject or accept the repressive texts. "When one defines the exercise of power as a mode of action upon the actions of others...one includes an important element: freedom" (Foucault, 1982, p. 789). And this freedom to reject the repressive text is crucial: "in order for power relations to exist there must be 'points of insubordination which, by definition, are means of escape'" (Foucault, 1982, p. 794). To reject the text of the classroom then, not only interrupts and threatens the coherency of established self-texts, but also, according to Foucault, the very expression of a relationship of power. I am confronted with and unable resolve the tension between the ways in which the knowledges available to me about teaching and children produce certain locations of power and prohibit others and my efforts to perform as "teacher." The moment passes.

Desire

By request, I am reading books to one of the children on the floor. She is sitting on my lap, stroking my hair, asking me questions about the details of the stories and the illustrations. I feel myself stiffen as she pets and rubs every part of my body. I continue to read the story which she has handed me. Impatient, she pulls the book from my hand, replacing it with another. She turns the pages more quickly than I can read them. I skim the pages, annotating the story, trying to match the speed of her interest. As she wiggles in my lap, I can feel my body fill with the desire for stillness, for quiet, for the opportunity to read to this child. She is, however, neither still nor quiet. I am unable to respond to her questions, read as quickly and sporadically, and respond to her touches at the same time. I feel that every bit of my space has been taken up by this child. I feel myself overwhelmed by what is being asked of me.

I am filled with conflictual feelings about my physical and emotional relationship with this child. As "teacher," I understand my relationship with children to be most certainly physical and emotional, as well as intellectual. The teaching relationship, however, has definitive boundaries. These boundaries are very much socially and culturally generated both in terms of a teacher's role and in interpersonal relationships generally. To be touched and spoken to in those ways felt totally unacceptable; I was being suffocated by her desire for interaction. Yet, to be available to the children whom I teach is an essential element of my "teaching." I equally want to be fulfill the child's desires. I felt caught between what I felt I should be giving the child and what I want for myself. She and I were caught in the chasm of desire, unable to either be fulfilled or escape.

Desire, as it is constructed as part of classroom discourse, for the most part, does not exist. It exists only in its absence, in the efforts of educational discourse to control and regulate it. When I speak of desire, I obviously do not simply mean sexual desire. Desire is that which moves our bodies, minds, and souls through space and time. Desire locates what we love and how we come to know about it. In the scientific discourse of modernist culture, desire is seen as a disruptive force, one which works against rationalist thought. Out of this negative dualism have been created complex cultural, political, and scientific systems to regulate the potentially devastating disruptions of desire.

The work of Michel Foucault (1980) on "the history of sexuality" looks specifically at the ways cultural, political, and economic forces in the nineteenth century worked to create a notion of "sexuality," that is, the existence of an locatable sexual identity, in order to regulate sexual behavior which fell outside cultural, political, and economic "standards." Part of this movement was to generate a regulating discourse around children's sexual (physical) behavior. The primary impetus of this discourse was to desexualize children as fully as possible. The work of Sigmund Freud (1962) is probably the most well known for his theory of sexual stages. This theory continues to have tremendous impact on the understanding of children's physical experiences. The preschool child's body has been all but erased by being located at the beginning of the "latency" period of Freud's continua. The most far-reaching effect has been to remove from children's lives the entirety of the discourse of desire, as desire can only be defined as adult sexuality. Children's bodies become the location of the first assault against the construction of the self as a desirous being. To what extent then, is the crisis of desire between me and the child not simply about space, but also about precisely what is allowable to desire?

The moment of tension surrounding desire should not only be seen as a crisis in asking and giving, however. Given the discourse surrounding desire in which we are operating, it is also crucial to recognize the importance of desire as an impetus of resistance. In an environment which is particularly predicated on the invisibility of desire, unrestrained desire marks an intense location. Although I cannot speak to the intentions of this child, I know that the persistence of her asking/wanting has the capacity to disrupt the coherency of the classroom text. I am rendered unable to continue to act as "teacher" in that I cannot interact with the child in a way that constitutes "teaching." I can neither continue to teach nor stop. This child has, in asserting her desire, made "teaching" impossible and I am lost, momentarily, in the excess of desire. The moment passes.

Voice

Another teacher and I stand near three children playing with play dough. The children are enjoying themselves, laughing and talking, experimenting with all the utensils provided with the dough. As they play, they watch us, glancing towards us between giggles. This is one of the first times that these three children have played together that we (the teachers) did not need to intervene repeatedly to settle disputes. I am half listening to what they are saying. I listen more carefully because I realize that I cannot understand what they are saying. They are using words which have no meaning to me, a fantastic language. I begin listening carefully. When the other teacher comments on what one of the children is making, the children respond in their "language," and laugh with great enthusiasm. She asks them what they are saying. They respond again in their non-language language and continue to laugh, even louder because we can't understand. It then becomes clear that they are "talking" about us. They look at us, one says one or two words and laughing begins. The dynamic between us intensifies.

I am impressed and amused by their engagement with the "language" as well as nervous, knowing that defiant, insulting words, even in a made up language, have serious meanings. They, too, have the ability to interrupt the "teacher" discourse which dominates the context of the classroom. This speaking however does not merely interrupt the text; it rewrites it: first creating a space in which to speak, then speaking about the very force which represses. As teachers we are engulfed by a crisis of the text: we are unable to speak to the children; our words no longer have meaning. Even more disturbing is that the children are generating their own meanings. Continuing to rely on the established and establishing texts, we have neither a way out (back into "our" texts) or in (into the children's texts). We are effectively suspended in discursive inaction.

Again, I do not want to argue that disruption was the *intent* of the children, rather, that it was, more importantly, the outcome. The effect of their actions is precisely what caused the crisis of voice, which, in a single moment, transfigured the structure of silence. In his work regarding popular culture, John Fiske (1989) has argued that this is exactly the task of "popular texts," that is, to undo and rewrite the oppressive texts of what he, drawing on the work of Stewart Hall, calls "the power bloc" (p. 28). He explains that the creation and use of popular texts are not only about the displacement of controlling texts, but also the pleasure experienced from production of such texts. If "our pleasure derives from the creating of the release from linguistic discipline," then it is surely evidenced in the children's unabashed enjoyment of the interaction. The disruption of the discourse of the classroom through the interruption and literal re-invention of the teacher-student text works powerfully to create a location from which to speak about silence, pleasure and power. The moment passes.

Epilogue: A Return to the Present

> One has to know one's buried truth in order to be able to live one's life. (Felman & Laub, 1992, p. 78)

We all have stories to tell, and, as Dori Laub (Felman & Laub, 1992) reminds us, "there is...an imperative need to *tell* and thus come to *know* one's story" (p. 78). And yet, many of our stories do not get told, the stories which form the crucial fabric of our lives, the stories which help us to survive. Even before I began to speak my "truths," I questioned the reliability of memory and language to successfully perform such tasks. There is much missing from the stories I tell of my teaching, even as try to "capture" and explore moments of particular import. Missing from these stories are the events which have come before to shape those moments: stories of previous teaching and learning experiences, stories of my own childhood, stories of loss and silence and struggle, stories which I cannot speak, possibly even to myself.

To wonder about our own silences as teachers, as reseachers, as women is to shift the conversation from the hearing to telling. It is to bring our own stories of transgression and borders and silences and speaking to the fore. It is to acknowledge the presence and absence of our own bodies and voices. This has been one of the (recent) great struggles of postmodern academics: to make present the visceral as well as the mindful voice, to explore the meaning of moving from the "one" to the "I."

In the opening section of this writing, I have offered some examples of the ways in which feminist teachers and researchers have struggled with the issue of presence and voice for some time. The absence and excess of the ways in which women's bodies and voices have been constructed has made this a compelling project for feminist writers, researchers and theorists whose very words are stake. Clearly, as women, we struggle against the constraints of language and politics to tell our stories, but what are the silences that are left by our own inability to tell or even to know our stories?

In *What Does a Woman Want?*, Shoshana Felman (1993) explores this point in by looking at the exclusions of her own story. Or more precisely, how she may speak her story only as it is disguised as the story of another. Her story, the story of a woman, is hidden to her and is revealed though the telling of the story of another. And moreover, the story with which she tells of the other is in fact motivated by the effort to speak her own story. She writes,

> ...if the critical suggestion I am making in this book is that people tell their stories (which they do not know or cannot speak) through others stories, then the very force of insight of this critical suggestion was at once borne out and actively enacted, put in motion, but the process of my writing which was driven, in effect, by the ways in which I was precisely missing my own implication in the texts before me. (1993, pp. 18-19)

Returning now to the promise and the challenge of teaching and telling the stories of children and classrooms, I must ask, how do we as researchers write the unavailable stories of children as we write the stories that are unavailable to us through them? Do we speak ourselves as ghosts in the stories of others? If so, how do we as women researchers, how do I as a researcher of young children, tell, write, and hear through the silences and displacements of all of our stories as they disappear and are rewritten as someone else's? What can we respond to our own inability to tell (even as I speak of my own inability to teach)? How do we make use of the crisis of speech and the crisis of silence?

I return to Peggy Phelan's (1993) insight that representation never conveys enough and always more than it intends. In other words, our attempts to represent experience are always doomed to fail both in their silences and excesses. The power of stories then, is not to *explain* experience, but to bring memory into the present in ways that it has not been before. Stories create the possibility *to tell* and *to know* the past and to reimagine the future even in the uncertainty of the present and the very stories we tell. Shoshana Felman (1992) writes, "The power of *narrative as testimony* is not merely to record, but to rethink and, in the act of its rethinking, in effect transform history by bearing literary witness…" (p. 95). It is the movement toward transformation that compels the work I do here as I writer, the work I do in a classroom as a teacher, and the work I do daily as a theorist and researcher. As women write the lives of others, we must hear the silences and excess of our own stories in order to continue to tell and transform the lives we speak through our teaching and research.

References

Ashton-Warner, S. (1963). *Teacher*. New York: Simon and Schuster.

Ashton-Warner, S. (1967). *Myself*. New York: Simon and Schuster.

Barthes, R. (1975). *The pleasure of the text*. New York: The Noonday Press.

Butler, J. (1990). *Gender trouble*. New York: Routledge.

Cochran-Smith, M., & Lytle, S.L. (1992). *Inside/outside: Teacher research and knowledge*. New York: Teachers Collge Press.

Felman, S. (1993). *What does a women want?: Reading and sexual difference*. Baltimore: Johns Hopkins University Press.

Felman, S., & Laub, D. (1992). *Testimony: Crisis in witnessing in literature, psychoanalysis, and history*. New York: Routledge.

Fiske, J. (1989). *Understanding popular culture*. Boston: Unwin Hyman.

Foucault, M. (1972). *The archaeology of knowledge and the discourse on language*. New York: Harper Colophon Books.

Foucault, M. (1979). *Discipline and punish: The birth of the prison*. New York: Vintage Books.

Foucault, M. (1980). *The history of sexuality: Volume I, and introduction*. New York: Vintage Books.

Foucault, M. (1982). The subject and power. In H. Dreyfus & P. Rabinow (Eds.), *Critical inquiry* (pp. 777-795). Chicago: University of Chicago Press.

Freud, S. (1962). In J. Streachey (Ed.). *Three essays on the theory of sexuality*. New York: Basic Books.

Grumet, M. (1988). *Bitter milk: Women and teaching*. Amherst: The University of Massachusetts.

hooks, b. (1989). *Talking back: Thinking feminist, thinking black*. Boston: South End Press.

Marshall, B. (1992). *Teaching the postmodern*. New York: Routledge.

Middleton, S. (1987). Schooling and radicalization: Life histories of New Zealand feminist teachers. *British Journal of Sociology of Education, 8*, 169-189.

Miller, J. (1992). Teachers, autobiography, and curriculum: critical and feminist perspectives. In *Reconceptualizing the early childhood curriculum*, B. Blue Swadner & S. Kessler (Eds.), (pp.103-122). New York: Teachers College Press.

Norquay, N. (1991, April). *The other side of difference: Memory-work in the mainstream*. Paper presented at the meeting of the American Educational Research Association, Chicago, IL.

Paley, V. (1979). *White teacher*. Cambridge: Harvard University Press.

Paley, V. (1992). *You can't say you can't play*. Cambridge: Harvard University Press.

Phelan, P. (1993). *Unmarked: The politics of performance.* London: Routledge.

Trinh, T. M. (1989a). Introduction. *Discourse, 11* (2), 5-17.

Trinh T. M. (1989b). *Woman, native, other: Writing, post-coloniality, and feminism.* Bloomington: Indiana University Press.

CHAPTER EIGHT

JANICE JIPSON
BRUCE WILSON

TH AT DIA LOG UE AT NI GHT

Jan:

I typed up our dialogue from Wednesday night and added a response to your last response. Don't expect very prompt responses to your side of the dialogue this way. When I have lots to do—like write a unit plan I don't check my e-mail very often. Then I hear from my siblings over the phone and they ask me if I have checked my e-mail lately. But I'll be seeing you on Wednesdays and we'll have to bring the latest correspondence with us. See you Monday.

—Bruce

Wednes day at ni ght

J: In the beginning, you intrigued me with your resistance to my syllabus which I thought was fairly student centered. And after thinking about it, I felt compelled to reposition myself to allow you to reconstruct the curriculum and/or assignments to meet your own needs. I had no choice. It was reasonable—a logical, acceptable example of what I believed. And yet it made me nervous. How different could I let you be?

(See, still in the script!) I wasn't letting you shake me up then—somewhere you started to do that—disturbing.

B: Well you allowed it. (See, still in the script!)

J: Allowed it? I enjoyed it!! What I wished more people would do—You can't abandon the script in a void—only in a relationship. So, I'm still curious about our new script—friends, collaborators—what are the restrictions each imposes? I was disappointed when you 'disappeared' semester two—I missed the challenge, felt blown off—retreated back to the teacher script. And then the **boycott**—the real pleasure in being made to look at teaching differently, the exploration of the unknown, the possibility within and at the edges of difference. So—am I still in the script?

Was I ever?

Or was that my imposter's rendering of the script?

For Sartre, one plays at a role in order to become the role, while in actuality no one is fully the role that he or she plays or seeks to assume. The 'public' demands that one act in a certain fashion, play a role in a certain way, but a person is not reducible to a role. —Mitchell Aboulafia, *The Meditating Self: Mead, Sartre, and Self-Determination*, p.28

Bruce: Who is this imposter that you are speaking of now?

J: Me—pretending to be the teacher. You see—
    I always am—just me.

B: I knew that.

J: So—why the fuss—am I that transparent?
        (I've been told so before.)
            Is this a game then of revealment?

B: Definitely!
    Especially if you subscribe to the definition of Self as something shared by all of us, rather than the reductionist view of self as millions of biological units simply attempting to survive this brief moment in time that we call a life.

J: Is it an unmasking? Then who is the performance for? And who is the self you are pretending not to be?

Carnival is the place for working out, in a concrete- ly sensuous half-real and half-play-acted form, *a new mode of interrela- tionships between individ- uals*—Bahktin, 1984.

The only way we know the world exists is because we perceive it. Vishva, the universe, in its truest sense exists as a relation- ship; the relationship between the perceiver and what is perceived, between the subject and object. A universe cannot be perceived unless there is someone there to perceive it, so in that sense the whole of creation as an object depends on the perceiving subject. The entire process of creation, therefore, is the manifesta- tion of perceiv- ing sentient beings and the objects of their experience. These sentient beings are the light of Chiti and they share one com- mon nature—the Self. So even though there are many perceivers, at the heart of each being there is only one universal Perceiver.

B: The performance is for the pure enjoyment of the self you are pretending not to be, and it is the pretender, the follower of scripts that asks who is the self that the pretender is try- ing not to be, or in psy- chological and mystical terms the pretender is the ego. And by asking who the self is, the ego objectifies what it pretends not to be; thereby maintaining the charade as it plays this game of Self revealment. But this is a long way from the immediate impulse for the boycott which was resistance to the syllabus assignment of writing a second edition of the philosophy of education paper that you asked us to write the first semester of the program. In a course titled "Integrated Curriculum" and with your reference the first day of class to emer- gent curriculum, and your constant stress on an authentic rela- tionship with students, and collaborative learn-

Only
because of
the acquired limita-
tions of a body,
mind and senses does
the Perceiver become
many limited subjects,
and then their experience
of the world becomes
many particular universes.
—Swami Shantananda

ing; the idea of sitting down and
writing, in isolation from my
cohort, my philosophy of education for an audience of one,
you the professor—
I felt so much contradiction
between what you espoused
verbally on the one hand
and the script you enact-
ed as teacher,
I felt short changed.

J: Sorry!
Well, you have
certainly told
me of your
philosophy.
Maybe   But who
it's not   positions
know-   whom in
ing who   this
you   script?
are—the
self you
pretend
not to be—
and the
performance
is to enact,
ironically all
those other
selves—to
play.

I
think
you
give me
too much
power as a
teacher.

In carnival everyone is an
active participant, everyone com-
munes in the carnival act...its participants live in it, they live by its laws as
long as those laws are in effect, that
is, they live a carnivalistic life. The
laws, prohibitions, and restrictions
that determine the structure and
order of ordinary, that is noncar-
nival life are suspended during
carnival; what is suspended first
of all is hierarchical structure
and all the forms of terror,
reverence, piety, and eti-
quette connected with it—
that is, everything resulting
from socio-hierarchical
inequality. All distance
between people is suspended and a special carnival category goes into effect: *free
and familiar contact among
people.*
—Bakhtin, again..

I think
you inscribe, and thereby limit,
my possibility.

B: The scary thing about emergent curriculum is that it is unpredictable and it doesn't respect boundaries—that is, emergent curriculum as I want to define it—in spite of its lack of respect for boundaries. I don't want to be limited by the definitions of curriculum that are currently the norm. If we want to get to a place where learning has **ultimate meaning** for the student—true student centered education—then we have to see the student as a whole person and the student's curriculum is her/his life, the context in which the individual student exists.

J: And the teacher, too?

B: What emerged for me as I faced your syllabus was the choice to boycott it.

My motivation for the boycott was the idea of crossing boundaries. We were positioned by the teacher-student boundary, you on one side and me on the other. I didn't want to obliterate the

J: Ultimate meaning? Do you mean personal meaning?

B: Ultimate meaning is an absolute experienced in a multiplicity of ways on a personal level. It is the means by which we come to self-affirmation or to the Self that we are pretending not to be.

"engaged pedagogy"…emphasizes well-being. That means that teachers must be actively committed to a process of self actualization that promotes their own well-being if they are to teach in a manner that empowers students.
—bell hooks,
Teaching To Transgress.

Are we exploiting the ambiguity of promise? xxxx:xvi.

B:
I am mixing an eastern philosophy with the theology of Paul Tillich and his concept of **ultimate concern**. There are many things that capture our concern in our effort to negotiate happiness. The objects of these concerns are often peripheral to real happiness. We experience them as the "conditions" of happiness. We concern ourselves with contingencies when we might be closer to our goal exploring the depths of our concern.

boundary in terms of the roles we each had, but I did want us to visit each other—cross boundaries back and forth—in terms of the script prescribed by the roles. I wanted to open up a dialogue that was not completely dictated by the roles. In the context of my personal history, having been involved with a small group of Caesar Chavez's followers in the early 70's boycotting grapes and Gallo wine, as well as picketing grocery stores that sold those products, a boycott was the natural response. If you disagree with the actions of a large institution or corporation, you boycott their product and picket the production and sale of that product. So I called you

J: But how can we assume any conditions to happiness when that would be to deny possibility—as if happiness really existed in only the one place or within one self.

Do we know how happiness is? A state of being? Personally arranged? Or better yet, perhaps, as pleasure experienced in a moment of surprise.

B: Sounds like operant utilitarianism. There is a paradox to the spatial metaphor I'm using for happiness. The image of happiness as something within us to be discovered conjures up something CONTAINED. But it is the contingencies we create, the conditions we demand for our happiness that is the attempt to contain or possess. We are incessantly grasping for the objects of concern which we feel will capture our happiness. Ultimate concern expands the horizons of our vision beyond the reach of our grasp.

that Sunday afternoon and told you
[to] *"collaborate in a discussion*
I was going to boycott your class.
that crosses boundaries and
And I told you that I wanted you to
create a space for intervention.
sanction the boycott, which was my way
of inviting you to play.
It is fashionable these days...."
It was a way for me to frame my feelings of resistance
(hooks, (1994), p. 129).

Now obviously if this was a boy-cott to take on the university and state of California, I wouldn't have asked you to sanc-tion my boycott. I wouldn't need and I certainly wouldn't want your sanctioning of it. I wouldn't see you as understanding or favoring my position at all. Boycotts and pickets are usually hostile engagements of those one opposes. But with my experience with you the first semester of the program when I resisted the first syllabus in a less direct manner, I knew from those conversations that you would likely want to play with this idea of a boycott. I was inviting you into a new conversation which was new and familiar at the same time. It was new in the sense that I was taking a more public vocal and visible stance in opposition to the way you were conducting the class than I did the first semester, and it was familiar in that we were taking up some of the same issues we discussed that first semes-ter of the program. And as I told you a few weeks into this current semester, I was unhappy with the product that I handed in to you that first semester, that collection of short stories which I called *The Zen of Inquiry*. I felt it was somehow unfinished. Now I look at it as a trial run for this semester's boycotting the script. I was testing the

in a manner that would effectively engage your attention and at the same time, open up possibility for exploration of the script we both felt com-pelled to follow because of our roles as student and professor.

Empty transgression, image of the move-ment of every trans-gression that nothing prohibited precedes, but which also does not place the limit by the crossing of the uncrossable. —Blanchot (1992), p. 106.

By imagina-tive acts of substi-tution we repress and replace whatever has been unaccept-able. ibid, 65.

waters that first semester, getting to know you and see how you would respond to me.

With that behind me, I started this semester with a sense of who you are and what you are about. That enabled me to approach you with less trepidation and more playfulness— thus the boycott. Coupled with the sense of something left undone that first semester and my 'disappearing,' so to speak, the second semester when I had no classes with you, I can understand your questions about what happens after the present semester is over. But we have much work to do in our weekly meetings reconstructing our dialogues which are for me much more interesting than sitting in the back of the room picketing with my **"Boycott the Script"** picket sign.

The fact that people tend to flirt only with serious things—madness, disaster, other people—makes it a relationship, a way of doing things, worth considering. —Phillips, p. xvii.

J: Do you have to have a script? What about free play? The allowance of the indeterminate?

But our preference for progress narratives can make flirtation acceptable only as a means to a predictable end. —Phillips, p. xvii.

B: It just occurred to me, this idea has been with me from the beginning, that I am boycotting the script, not the roles. I don't see us changing the script of professor-student. It is not a matter of changing the script, but rather allowing a dialogue to emerge, regardless of the roles.

Dear Bruce:
I thought I would type up our conversation. Please read and edit this in the spirit of constructive play. I hope this makes sense. It is, after all, infinitely editable and you will have the disk. —Jan

J: Does all this stuff we've been reading about the carni-

valesque, mysticism, etc. provide the tension for our play?
I think it is the teasing out of the plot, the flirtation with
the ideas, the delays that increase the tension, enhance
the value.

B: But is it narcissistic? Can our experiences be generalized? Are they too personal? Is it just a mutual admiration
society?

J: Or a healthy narcissism? Positive self regard starts, after
all, with the other/the mother. So, then, our carnival/boy-
cott is an inversion—a dream of a classroom, a Nut-
cracker Suite where the wooden toy soldier becomes the
hero and the little girl can be a princess after all. And
patriarchy takes on its sadistic persona and can be van-
quished—but of course that is all a dream and eventually
Marie wakes up, as do we all. So does the tension pro-
long the dream? Is that what this is about? Maintaining a
state of irreality?

B:
And is it play/full tension   (B: I didn't ask this question, but
or unbearable tension/   that's o.k. The idea about *tension for*
sadism?   *the play* came up when you noted
                              that I referred to you as my professor
                          when telling others about this project. I
                      said that I thought that maintaining the role dis-
                  tinction was a way of maintaining the tension for the play—
that it was the motor of our interaction. I said I might continue to
refer to you as my professor even after graduation to tease out all of
the meaning in that relationship.

Recently, I am beginning to think we are collaborators and feeling that if a learning community is to come out of the boycott, it
should be an evolution of our dialogue about boycotting the script. I
am feeling less inclined on my own to initiate a learning community,
because our dialogue seems to have become the center around
which so many ideas are gravitating. It makes more sense to me for
both of us to expand our dialogue to include others and allow a
learning community to emerge.

Our dialogue has a certain feeling of irreality to it, because it is
such a different way of approaching a university course and conse-

quently may be a surrealistic acting out of our roles as student and professor. We have begun a dialogue about the idea of curriculum as 'world' and about the integration of that world through the crossing and recrossing of boundaries which prescribe our roles as student and professor—until the boundaries have become so trampled that they almost cease to exist. The closest we came to enacting the traditional roles was the day I was sitting at your computer in your office working on these pages as you graded unit plans and you turned to me and asked what grade I wanted.)

We are wrong to believe that the true and the false paradoxically can only be brought to bear on solutions…. It is the school teacher who "poses" the problems; the pupil's task is to discover the solutions. In this way we are kept in a kind of slavery. True freedom lies in a power to decide, to constitute problems themselves. The truth is that in philosophy and even elsewhere it is a question of finding the problem, consequently of positing it even more than solving it. For a speculative problem is solved as soon as it is properly stated. By that I mean that its solution exists then, although it may remain hidden and, so to speak, covered up: The only thing left to do is to uncover learning. But stating the problem is not simply uncovering, it is inventing, actually or virtually; it was therefore certain to happen sooner or later. Invention gives being to what did not exist; it might never have happened. —Deleuze on Henri Bergson, *Cinema 1, The Movement-Image.* p.15-16.

B: How do we devise a setting for the play of our students (with us, with ideas, with stuff)? How do we construct tensions for our students to play in?

J: Is this the script? A Five-Easy-Piece Tension?

B: I did ask this one. What we have done is recognize a dilemma, the inhibitions to learning that are inherent in a hierarchical, (unitized and semester-ized) institution of learning and dared to step outside of it to encounter each other as persons. We did this in the context of our roles as student and professor. Our roles were the motor for our dialogue—our emergent curriculum about integrated curriculum.

B: But—can our experiences be too personal? Can they be generalized to other people? To a learning community? To a community of people not like us?

J: Is the value in the therapeutic—self knowledge, exploration, possibility? Or is the value in the pure pleasure of the play? Or, maybe, is the value in the creative process?—spinning gold from straw and late night meanderings? (Does the accidental, occasional nature of it make it all the more lustrous?) Does the glow it creates lighten our classrooms and our world? Is that what art is about? Or teaching?

[A man and a woman enter a small, brightly lit neighborhood Thai restaurant in a low-end strip mall...the waitress gestures them to the rear of the room.]

B: So...the usual curry? I'm hungry tonight— lets get 2 dishes. Now, how are we going to begin this paper?

J: Well, I see fragments strewn about on a page. A collage of semi-transparent, brightly colored, tissue paper carelessly, almost randomly, arranged—overlapping, colliding, merging, changing as they glow through each other's intensity—kind of like our conversations here—no apparent order or pattern, but certainly circling around some common concerns and interests we have.

But what story do we tell?

B: Well, the subject is the boycott, but the form it takes alludes to Jung and dreams and tarot and muses. And in telling the story we enact our point which is that the hierarchical, linear forum leaves out the play of the muses, the imagination, the multiplicity of consciousness.

Is it that "ethography, like fiction, constructs existing or possible worlds....[and] no matter its pretense to present a self-contained narrative or cultural whole remains incomplete and detached from the realms to which it points"? —Kamala Visweswaran (1994) *Fictions of Feminist Ethnography.*

J: It's a non-sense discourse with fragmented incursions of meaning. It's the mundane of classroom management next to poetic, integrated, even political con

Is it "a non-narrative narrativity?" —Deborah Britzman (1994)

B: We want to create feeling but not the literal image of what happened with the boycott—

versation. It's transitory, partial, fragmented. Like I said before, it's an array of gems.

it's like we're stalking affect. We're telling a story, a conversation to tie the fragments together.

J: And if we talk nonsense, the narrative is told by the juxtaposed pieces. But I'm not sure how to get that image on paper and still have it make some sense to the reader. But does it have to make sense? If the reader makes the sense of it, maybe we don't have to take responsibility for that, just position the images so that

Is it about "our preference for progress narratives?" —Adam Phillips (1994), (p. xvii).

we can "read" them and let the reader construct her own sense of it—kind of like a massive, disorderly, verbal Rorschach of ideas, I guess. You're the artist, you tell me...

More tea—and make sure it is really hot this time.

B: Another question...is this daredevil research?
What's risky about it?
The chaos of the form we allow?

J: I see it as a challenge to the cultural scripts for doing research. We literally make spaces for our ways of doing inquiry. If only we could somehow contain this dinner table conversation and flip it onto the paper without loosing the sometimes jittery, random flow— the juxtapositions, the possibilities.

But, about this boycott—the multiple boycotts that you have imposed, actually, and which I've sanctioned, albeit sometimes quite reluctantly. It seems to me that in engaging in the boycott script (of boycotting the scripts) and in stepping outside the familiar, pushing at the boundaries of the usual ordained academic discourse, we have created our own carnival or dream state. Sometimes I wonder if it is not a nightmare, after all—the potentially sadistic turns it could take as we wrestle with the power issues. What was that dream you mentioned the other night? An evil spirit stalking you, your mantra providing a screen to protect yourself? That is pretty powerful—another boycott of sorts.

Looking for a significant meal, the bird of prey returns to the territory- of a previous hunt.

B: I remember well the dream, but the specific tension I spoke of that night is a bit vague. I believe it was about the inherent antagonism in the autonomous and free voice so frequently silenced by the 'cultural scripts' played out in societal roles. I compared student response to the syllabus to the filling of invoices in the warehouse of knowledge.

10:18 p.m. Saturday, December 11, 1993. You might be wondering why I haven't said much about classroom culture. I did all those interviews and read pages of material to try and arrive at some definition or description of classroom culture, and... My conclusion is that each individual must define it for him/herself. The key to understanding classroom culture is the hearing of each individual's stories. For me classroom culture is not the filling of invoices, but the filling in of voices.
It's all about dialogue.
It's all about person centered education, whether that person is the student, the teacher, or the parent. It's about interacting as persons rather than playing roles.

B: Do you want dessert?

B: I want mine cold.

J: Tapioca— warm

J: This was the best hot chocolate I ever had, by the way. She said "Do you like it really chocolatey?" And I said "Yeah. I hate thin chocolate, I hate thin coffee. **This is terrific.**"

B: Well thin hot chocolate or thin coffee…It has no…

J: Body.

B: Yeah, that's right, not rich.
    A lot of conversations are like that.

J: Exactly. For me, that's been a central benefit
        of this boycott business
        —the opportunity for rich hot chocolate.

B: I like the mood of this place.
    It shifted when those two guys over there left. I don't
know what they were talking
about…but this music is fine and the
voices of the people still scattered about
blends with it and is very soothing…the
music, the voices, the hum of the
beverage coolers. What I am trying to
convey is a contentment with whatever I
am in the present moment—with a subtle
sense of possibility—a centeredness that
breathes in the environment without any
judgments that are readily released—to
stay centered and ready or open to
insight. It's the way of Vipassana, the
Buddhist meditative practice.

"The mythology of the celebration contains the inversion of daily life in its development…it is not simply a matter of getting unusual pleasure but of pushing them to their very limit…the break with tempo of work…the festival is upside down; Everything happens backwards…" —Cixous (1975), p. 22.

J: Yes, I also like the feeling of this
place, the music, the pulse of the
writing—words not lost in the saying—

B: As you were writing, I was contemplating how we
began our conclusion. It seems that what we have done
is to pay homage to the gods that inhabit this place in
their various forms, sights and sounds. We have paid
homage by our willingness to be here with them without
getting caught up in our own purpose or direction. We

have let the local gods "talk" to us and created a sacred space. I think Thomas Moore has written about this in his *Care of the Soul*. I think narratives always lead away from the center. We are taken on an adventure away from ourselves. But if we take the trip with a certain kind of detachment, playfully, we can reap the pure pleasure of movement without getting so caught up in the drama that we are completely eaten up (or do I mean, frightened off) by the various gods of whatever locality we occupy at the time. We stay in touch with the center and are nourished by the insights gained from the joys and pains of the journey.

> Like creatures in fairy tales, we've shrunk and we've swollen we've swallowed the cosmos whole.
> —Mukherjee, 1989, p. 214

J: There are many playings, and it is an interesting idea that the gods of the/any place conjure us up. Actually, I prefer divine intervention—it relieves some of the responsibility. This process, however, sometimes engulfs me in confusion. I realize the tentative limits of my understanding.

B: Well, I have had about all the conclusion I can stand for now. Why don't we analyze our data?

J: Aiming for insight, no doubt—now we are on more treacherous ground—the rules allow for divergence, multiplicity and the inevitable multiple regressions—are you ready for that? Analysis is generative after all—does not preclude choice, change, options, growth, regeneration.

B: What rules? Whose rules?

J: Caught again
—the idea that all possibility
is entertained until proven otherwise.
And since we are beyond the conclusion,
all possibility is entertained endlessly
—this opens the writing to wondering,
the journey round again.
It allows playfulness, possibility,
irony, humor—safer ground.

> B: Analysis is movement: This is where the joys and
> pain come in. If we can stay centered it will be
> pure pleasure. Otherwise…

J: I'm so distracted sometimes that
I mis-recognize the center. Whose center, anyway?

B: You have to find your own.
But in the end there is only one.

> J: Suggesting that I haven't yet?
> Or you haven't noticed me
>   there anyway.
>   And who allowed you to go first?

> > B: There you go again. Our analysis is the story
> > of our journey. Not the literal story but
> > what was it you suggested earlier?

> > > J: The metaphoric meaning of the boycott—
> > > the opening up of the non-linear, uncon-
> > > tained narrative of possibility, discovery—
> > > when we agree

to step aside from the conventions of the script (whatever script) we have the opportunity to invent all the risks, the discovery beyond. When we remind ourselves to deny convention, we can play—the script/story emerges not from expectation or past experience but from the shifting energy of the moment. That is what the journey is to me— unanticipated, sometimes resisted, always provocative. It's the tumbling words as I try to listen.

Transgression is the affirmation of difference. It is the joyous play of that which can neither be held captive by the gaze of the Same nor relegated by the Same to the darknesss of the Other. Transgression speaks to the Same, but in a language whose phrases disturb without being wholly understood… **"Transgression, then is not related to the limit as black to white, the prohibited to the lawful, the outside to the inside, or as the open area of a building to its enclosed spaces. Rather, their relationship takes the form of a spiral, which no simple infraction can exhaust"** (Foucault 1977b, p. 35). And thus transgression is always at risk, always in danger of being either captured or exiled by the structure it seeks to disrupt.
   —May, *Between Geneology and Epistemology.*

B: What was I doing metaphorically that Sunday when I called you and told you I was going to boycott your course? It was about resistance to an entrenched way of looking at teaching and learning as an activity whose style and manner is solely determined by the professor-student script. I wanted a different way of conversing about the subject matter of the course.

J: Your Sunday call interrupted my complacency and provided an opportunity for change/thinking otherwise about what I was doing—which then opened me up to consider that everything could be considered or acted (enacted?) differently. Metaphorically, then, the boycott was a rupture in a carefully constructed and protective posture, and the waves of confusion are still pouring through. A different way of conversing, yes, as student and teacher—not just about teaching, but about living—and not just the professor/student script, but about finding/making a space to be.

I no longer considered these personal reactions internal noise.... Rather, I looked to my reactions as an indicator of general patterns for coping with the continuous threat of potential destruction.
—Reinharz, 1984, p. 336.

SATURDAY Flower Power Pizza

J: Pin-ball, beer, horoscopes, Erik's bored (always)—It's funny how the contexts of our lives shift and yet continually circle back to an echo of the past, the familiar—there is a welcome in the football game on the TV, the sound of the pinball game, the guys saying "YES!!!" It seems particularly "right" to write a scholarly paper here. One can be so caught up in the moment of being that one forgets that everyone else may be somewhere else. Is this what happens in teaching? We forget the other? The mysterious separateness of each of us allows the hopeful play, the dream of a difference, the refusal to enter the same old patterns, ever again.

This magical device, here, by which the world can be transformed from banality to magic in a trice.
—Joseph Campbell, *Primitive Mythology: The Masks of God*

B: Well, you are making quite an assumption here—I think—about where I might be. Yes? No?

J: The point is: Do I know? No!

B: Two beers?
   No, it's the interruption of last night's dialogue on

paper that has interrupted the flow. Looking at your final comment last night, "It's not just about teaching, it's about living and it's not just the professor/student script, it's about my finding/making a space." That is exactly the way I was feeling that first semester when I came into your office and told you I didn't want to follow your syllabus. I remember how frustrated I felt sometimes because on the one hand you seemed opened to my doing something else, and we had some great conversations but peppered with your comments that one thing or another that I had written would substitute for something on the syllabus. You were hearing me but you weren't. So I was a bit nervous when I turned in my semester project—*The Zen of Inquiry*—though I thought you would like it. I think I was a bit afraid you would be stumped for something in your syllabus to substitute for it.

J: It's "Them Bears." I didn't want you to know I didn't take the syllabus that seriously either. We didn't know each other well enough to trust each other—only to test, fencing, jabbing at what we really meant. I sensed your energy, but was reluctant to step (too far)

> the 'doers' who bridge the chasm that lies between the safe inadequacy of what they've been taught and the fulfillment that they uncertainly sense will exist on the other side. —Koller, 1983, p. 94.

from the script and experience misunderstanding—I didn't want to be conned. The Zen paper was terrific—I remember thinking as I read it—here's someone who is not afraid to encounter all of his worlds. And fitting the Zen into the syllabus was at least partially ironic—a play. Did I have to prove I was the teacher? What was fair? If I wasn't the teacher what else was left? However I responded to you, it was from the position of teacher and from my responsibility for you—

now it's shifted. I think of my responsibility as being to
you—not that it's any (or much) clearer.

> a capacity...to attend to another person
> and to feel related to that person
> in spite of what may be enormous differences.
> —Belenky, et al., 1986, p. 143.

Last fall I could be bemused/amused by your work—and
with the Zen and the "Colonization of Students" paper for
my book, I was impressed—and now with this project, I
find myself beset with formless questions.
     The work is important.

> B: It is important for me to understand what
> that shift was that you are talking about—
> from your "responsibility for me" to "respon-
> sibility to me." I think we both are very curi-
> ous about that. And I shifted from a tentative
> kind of engagement with you the first
> semester of the program to a more self con-
> fident playing at boycotting the script in the
> final semester. Now instead of my attempt-
> ing to make a space for me to be, we both
> are playing at making a space for both of us
> to work in.

J: So, no longer taking responsibility for your learning, I
now take responsibility "with" you for learning—figuring
this paper out together—and the "with" implies a whole
set of new concerns—like allowing you your space and
whatever goes with that. By your self confident 'play' this
semester I can begin to engage more honestly, too—
more risks—your confidence allows me to also be more
confident, although, in other ways it makes me even
more tentative. It seems necessary to step outside of the
university—the official classroom—my office—learning to
live in each other's worlds. And maybe that is another
thing the boycott is—of the constraints of place—of

being able to center oneself and play, wherever. I think I've gone past 'sanctioning', however, and that is what this playing with (responsibility with?) is all about—sanctioning and boycotting imply oppositions and now, hopefully, with the semester over the boycott can shift to the expectations, habits, apologies and limits from our past experiences. In agreeing to play, to enter the carnival, to turn everything back on itself, it seems we must call into question all that is apparent or predictable. So the inquiry goes beyond reflection or analysis, but I'm not sure to what.

> I awake at 5:47 a.m. with clenched teeth. I don't understand these kinds of mornings when I awaken to find my flesh pleading with my bones not to abandon me. My bed offers no comfort on mornings like this. I may as well be lying on concrete.
> —Wilson, *Zen of Inquiry*

References

Aboulafia, M. (1986). *The mediating self: Mead, Sartre, and self-determination.* New Haven: Yale University Press.

Bakhtin, M. (1984). *Problems of Dostoevsky's poetics.* Minneapolis: University of Minnesota Press.

Belenky, M., Clinchy, B., Goldberger, N., & Tarule, J. (1986). *Women's ways of knowing: The development of self, voice and mind.* New York: Basic Books.

Blanchot, M. (1992). *The step not beyond.* Albany: SUNY Press.

Britzman, D. (1994). *On refusing explication: A non-narrative narrativity.* Paper presented at the meeting of the American Educational Research Association, New Orleans, LA.

Campbell, J. (1969). *Primitive mythology; The masks of God.* New York: Penguin Books.

Cixous, H. (1975). *The newly born woman.* Minneapolis: University of Minnesota Press.

hooks, b. (1994). *Teaching to transgress: Education as the practice of freedom,* New York: Routledge.

Deleuze, G. (1986). *Cinema 1: The movement-image.* Minneapolis: University of Minnesota Press.

Koller, A. (1983). *An unknown woman.* New York: Bantam.

May, T. (1993). *Between geneology and epistemology.* University Park, PA: Pennsylvania State University Press.

Moore, T. (1992). *Care of the soul.* New York: Harper Collins.

Mukherjee, B. (1989). *Jasmine.* New York: Ballantine Books.

Phillips, A. (1994). *On flirtation.* Cambridge: Harvard University Press.

Reinharz, S. (1984). *On becoming a social scientist.* New Brunswick, NJ: Transaction.

Shantananda. (1987). Pratyabhijnahrdayam: The recognition of the self, Part II. *Darshan. 9.,* 87-101.

Tillich, P. (1951). *Systematic theology: Volume one.* Chicago: The University of Chicago Press.

Visweswaran, K. (1994). *Fictions of feminist ethnography.* Minneapolis: University of Minnesota Press.

CHAPTER NINE

NICHOLAS PALEY

NEITHER LITERAL
NOR CONCEPTUAL

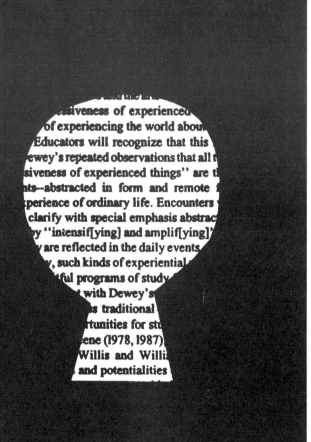

...iveness of experienced...
...of experiencing the world about...
...Educators will recognize that this...
...ewey's repeated observations that all t...
...siveness of experienced things'' are t...
...nts—abstracted in form and remote f...
...perience of ordinary life. Encounters...
...clarify with special emphasis abstrac...
...y "intensif[ying] and amplif[ying]"...
...y are reflected in the daily events...
...y, such kinds of experiential...
...tful programs of study...
...t with Dewey's...
...s traditional...
...rtunities for st...
...ene (1978, 1987)...
...Willis and Willi...
...and potentialities...

Only

an image

"waiting

for

our

return"?

it.

...ink I syste... ...y early rea...
...ly count... ...d "real"
at Belo... ...rd influence is i... ...ant be... ...trated
...tory. T... ...ative literature and a... ...exp... ...like
the im... ...rly the works of mode... ...ters,
...y–part... ...realists like Breton, S... ...It da...
...ts an... ...m these encounter...
...rima... ...a page in a mu... ...ty of...
...display... ...es can...
...express... ...ons that lite...
...terest in the con...
...tice began during my years
...tal graduate work in...

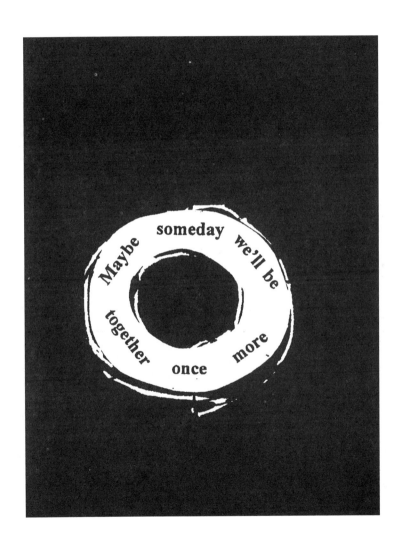

mport
conceptuall
oices. Overall, a   2 stud
uate) agreed to partic   this s

Analysis

ata analysis, each of us independently rea
es. We deliberately chose not to analyze
ny predetermined model that categorized
respo   ferring instead to provide the
by re   attentive to key themes and
fro   arratives. As we examined
identify patterns of literary choices and the
individual student lives, we found that
distinct categories which corresponded t
ate populations. To illuminate the comple
by students and their discussions of them,
ection, selected examples of undergrad
sponses. Several   esented in extende
deeply the patter   d themes evidence
s well as to provid   ght into the actual

Can anything that enters
this room have only its own
meaning ever again?
(Galway Kinnell)

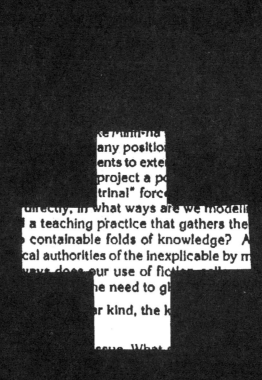

se/multi-na

any position

ents to exter

project a po

trinal" force

directly, in what ways are we modeli

a teaching practice that gathers the

containable folds of knowledge? A

cal authorities of the inexplicable by m

ways does our use of fiction

e need to g

r kind, the k

ssue. What

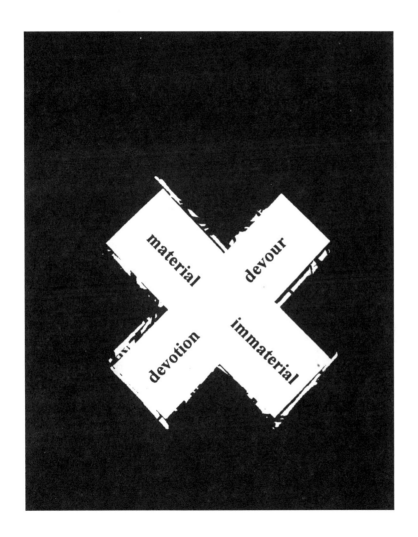

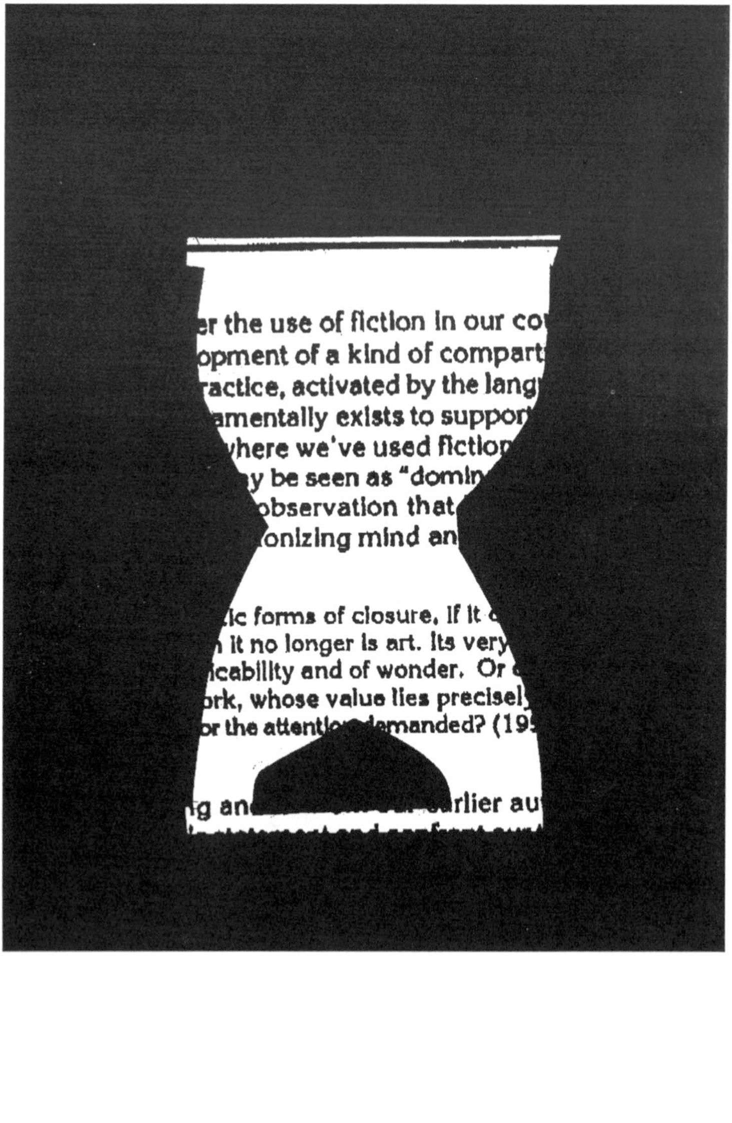

er the use of fiction in our co
opment of a kind of compart
actice, activated by the lang
amentally exists to support
here we've used fiction
y be seen as "domin
observation that
onizing mind an

ic forms of closure. If it
it no longer is art. Its very
icability and of wonder. Or
ork, whose value lies precisel
or the attention demanded? (19

g an earlier au

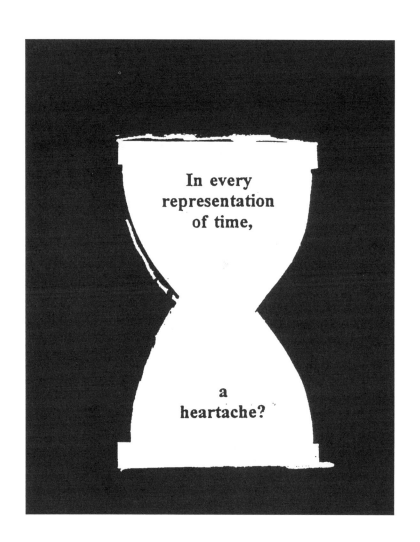

In every
representation
of time,

a
heartache?

Words as media ...
...ossibility. Noun...
...ions—that is to say character. ...
...enote character in its limitations ...
...ion. Words attempt to convey the ...
...hat they can convey character, n...
...al form, but as exhibited and operating in indi...
...vident in the novel and drama, whose business ...
...his particular function of language. For character...
...a situations that evoke their natures, giving particularity...
...xistence to the generality of potentiality. At the same time ...
...ituations are defined and made concrete ... Ethical treatises in ...
...he past have been impotent in comparison [to literature] in ...
...ortraying characters so that they remain in the consciousness ...
...f mankind. (Dewey 1958, 243)

education of

e house on mang stree
e call of stories: Teaching

he silenced dialogue: Power an
ard Educational Review, 58, 3
58). Art as experience. New Y
979). The grand inquisitor o
Educational Publishing.
gination and education. Ne
ching as story telling. Lond
. The joys of motherhood. N
dscapes of learning. N
worlds in schools. Jou
s. (in) Made from th
e of life: Other dim

anet of Junior Brown
l0la). The selective tra
in the elementary classi

991b). Is there a base to

DECONSTRUCTING WO/MENTORING

DIVING INTO THE ABYSS

Reconstructing Research
A Conversation with Thelma and Louise

Jan: You're not going to give up, are you?

Petra: What do you mean?

Jan: You're not going to make a deal? I just want to
know.

Petra: I'm not making any deals.

Jan: I mean, I'd understand if you would. In a way, you
got something to go back to—academic respectability
and all.

Petra: It's not an option.

Jan: But, uh, I don't know, you know, something's like
crossed over in me, and I can't go back. I mean I just
couldn't live.

Petra: I know. I know watcha mean. Anyway, I don't

want to end up on the damn Geraldo show.

Crunchy granola—you know.[1]

Jan: Yeah.

Petra: Uh, they're charging us with insurrection.

Jan: Ooohhhh…

Petra: Yeah, they say we have to figure out if we want to come in dead or alive.

Jan: Gosh, did they say anything positive at all?[2]

Mapping Friendship

Petra: Women's friendships. There are few images, few pictures of exploring what friendships between women mean. More often than not we see images of women competing against one another or re-enacting a male plot. Yet, in *Thelma and Louise*, the usual portrayal of women betraying women is disrupted. Thelma asks Louise if she is going to make a deal. Louise responds that she is not making any deals. The betrayal of the mother for the father does not take place.[3] The refusal to give in to patriarchy, to betray the "other" is incomplete. Louise reminds Thelma that they have to figure out if they want to come in dead

---

[1] Gregory Cizel (1995) uses the term "crunchy granola" in an essay exploring issues related to the increasing focus on narrative and qualitative research strategies in education.

[2] This research project emerged out of an ongoing friendship between the two authors which began in 1989 as a dissertation advisor (Jan) and doctoral student (Petra) relationship. The project is based on an audio-transcription of a dialogue between the authors in the summer of 1992. In presenting women's voices as pure text, as lived experience, the authors hope to disrupt the commonly held relegation of women's talk to "gossip."

[3] Traditional psychoanalytic theory maintains that female gender identity is predicated on the transference of the "love object" from the mother to the

or alive. It seems either way they are dead. If they "come in" patriarchy will have it's way; if they refuse they will always be on the run. The choice is really an artificial one—there is no real choice, just the illusions of rational, western, male thought.

Although the conclusion of the movie when Thelma and Louise plunge into the canyon might be seen as a tragic end, I remember the exhilaration I felt as I watched the ending of this film. Thelma and Louise's resistance, becomes an act of agency. Yet, my exhiliration is dampened by the realization that either death or insanity has traditionally been women's recourse in a man's world. I think of Kate Chopin's *The Awakening*, Charlotte Perkins Gilman's *The Yellow Wallpaper*, Edith Wharton's, Virginia Woolf, Sylvia Plath...women who struggled to name themselves, to claim their realities in a world in which the roles for women are severely prescribed. They do not give up on life, but return to and connect with nature, that which has always *represented women*.

At the heart of this movie is the friendship between two women. It was after watching the movie that I realized how few representations there are that address women's friendship.[4] I began to think about the roles women have played in my survival, helping to maintain my sanity. It seemed to me that the greatest gift two women could give each other was an acknowledgement that their feelings are real. Isn't that what it is all about?

---

father. Rejection of the mother for the father is necessary for what is considered to be normal sexual identity. It is against this domninant cultural plot that we explore what it means for women to sever their relationships with women in favor of the patriarchal position or, conversely, to value them despite cultural conditioning. We join Marianne Hirsch (1989) in examining what gender relations might be if not predicated on the normative "family plot."

[4] *Fried Green Tomatoes* and *Boys on the Side* are other recent examples.

No Boundaries:
Disrupting Geneology

(Holiday Inn, Evanston, Illinois
Summer, 1992)

Petra: ...getting back to our mentoring and our relationship...I mean when I switched advisors and decided
to work with you that was very difficult...I knew intu-
itively that it was the right thing. I just had a sense, a
feeling that it was the right thing to do. I can't say that
it wasn't a difficult choice for me. For me to choose a
woman mentor was a risky thing. A women dissertation advisor who was elementary and early childhood.
I think the thing I got most out of it was this sort of
unbridled path that you seem to facilitate. You know,
there were no boundaries, no bars, I guess with other
faculty, as I think about it now, there was this set
intellectual path that you were supposed to follow
and that meant following their train of thought, their
philosophical and intellectual interests.

I don't think my decision to work with you was solely
your interest in feminist theory or curriculum,
although that was certainly part of it. It was that there
were no constraints on my explorations—no matter
how fragmented or how disorganized I was as I
explored a lot of different areas...women's history,
curriculum theory, feminist theory, anthropology..., it
was all okay. That might have been interpreted by
other people as not being focused, that it was really
that unbridled...

Jan: Yes. But you see, first you have the right to do that
and secondly, that's what I do, too. I love the excite-
ment of being able to just charge into these
things...watch the foam spray up...the lack of fear of
intellectual adventure. I criticize myself for reading all

over the place and for going to the book store and for not knowing whether to go to anthropology, or literary criticism or women's studies or children's books or psychology or English.

Petra: Yeah, in some ways there is this bizarre aspect of academic mentoring that for men...your graduate students are your children. They are your product.

Jan: Forever.

Petra: They are the people who carry on your ideas and who establish you. That's another sort of subtle thing...that I've picked up on. Because what people talk about in terms of who has status in the academic community is how many graduate students did we have that went on and made it? That's a measure of your success. Especially in terms of male professors who can't birth their own children. It's their graduate students who become their children. It's a bizarre reversal of, you know, the traditional mothering thing but it's really them. They are the fathers sending their children out into the world to make a name for them.

Jan: At times I wished that I could cross that bridge and be more directive because it would be a lot easier on me to tell people what to do rather than to ask questions and let them discover what they wanted.

Petra: But on the other hand, with male professors and advisors it's very clear what the issues of control are. The issues of control aren't so apparent with men because it's so obvious what the relationship is going to be. But when the relationship transits the traditional boundaries it can become confusing.

"It's not just being smart"

Petra: As a male, you don't even question your capabilities because who you are in the world...is the right way and is validated by your sex...just because you are a man. That is never our experience.

Jan: Well, I think men, at least some men, if they are smart enough to pass the tests, whatever...the Miller's or the GRE or the grade point average to get in, then they don't doubt their belonging and they don't see that they don't have the other attributes which are necessary to survive.

It's not just being smart. It's other things that you have to do. For women, I think they are immense. God, no woman should have to be dependent on pleasing a man yet again, in order to survive. But to get back to the thing of mothering, I don't see it as mothering, but I see the relationship with students as caring about and caring for and part of that is to give them those things which you have. Frequently that is special knowledge or special skills. That has always been hard for me because my whole construction of my identity has been as the woman as nurturer...I go back historically to my great, great grandmothers...the women in my family were all very independent. They were the ones who supported the family as nurses or missionaries or teachers or...in a service kind of thing. One's worth-while-ness came from the "charity" that you did in your work with other people, not in who you were by yourself. You were known for your good works, by your relationship with other people.

Petra: I don't know. For me, with mentoring, I don't see it with that mother metaphor. It's interesting now that I have ended my first year as a professor...how do I see my role as mentor now that I am on the other end of things. I guess the thing that always comes up again and again for me is the sense of responsibility— not in terms of duty, you know, not like something that I have to do. But it's a sense of responsibility in terms of passing on what has been given to me...so there really is a generational passing on or sharing of the knowledge of what I've gotten about surviving in the academic world.

Jan: With me, I felt that I received little intentional mentorship outside of my formal academic training in college. It was my responsibility to teach myself how to do those things, but I was never quite sure what they were. And when I came to the University of Oregon—that was my first priority, to provide the mentoring for women students that I never quite got.

I felt it was my responsibility to do that because the chances for women to successfully survive the university system and conquer the tenure obstacles were severely limited by not knowing how to do those things. It took me years to discover how to get articles published on my own. I had to learn how to do it myself. The other thing that I really wanted...it was my agenda for change...was to bring women effectively into the university system so that they weren't dependent on the patronage of the male senior professors but were strong in and of themselves and able to function effectively. The way to do that, I felt, was to give them the skills before they ever went out so that they would be on their feet running when they started their first jobs.

Petra: Well, I guess for me, the thing about mentoring is that I think I ultimately get as much out of the mentoring relationships as the students. But, in some ways, it's not like I am giving and the other person is receiving. For me to really connect with somebody, it's got to be a two way street.

Jan: I think that also goes back to relationships—having an ongoing relationship with someone allows you to know them and get to the heart of their concerns and talk with them. Again, we write well together because we know each other so well and therefore can be critical of each other's work and, because of the trust inherent in the relationship, we can also be critical in a positive sense. We seem to know what the other person is trying to say because we know each other.

Petra: Exactly.

Jan: So, I can ask a question that doesn't become alien, but rather, it becomes facilitative. That's the importance of continuity in relationships.

Petra: It gets back to something that was such a problem for me in our research group, I want that criticism.[5] To me that's a sign of respect, that's a sign that somebody understands who I am. Exactly what you were saying, you know each other well enough that you know what that person is about and what they are trying to achieve from what philosophical base they are coming. You know them well enough and care enough to really get that criticism...constructive criticism. That's something that very few people are capable of doing.

Jan: What I see is a facilitator role where I can respond to individual needs and provide a safe environment to explore questions, focus on issues, all outside of the traditional academic environment. It's something that I don't think men are as able to do. The mentoring doesn't have to be hierarchical in terms of status. It has to be based on respect and care regardless of status. The whole idea is that if knowledge is socially constructed it doesn't have to occur with someone who has more knowledge, it has to be with someone

---

[5] Jan and I were also part of a larger women's research and study group from 1989–1991. This larger group experience also raised many issues regarding collaboration for us. They are documented in *Repositioning Feminism and Education: Perspectives on Educating for Social Change* (1995).

who has as much commitment to the process.

"Women like guys with ties"

Jan: When I was a graduate student, I sought out advisors and professors who were women and never quite believed, although I have had male professors, that men could mentor me in the same way. I thought that a woman would be better able to understand the intricacies of my experience as a woman. Particularly when I went back for my doctoral program, I initially only considered women advisors, and then I ended up with a man, anyway, because of our shared subject matter interest. I wanted someone who could understand what it was like for women in academic environments. I think what I was looking for was an individual with whom I wouldn't have to submerge my self doubts, with whom I could be honest, hoping they would understand the sources of my doubts and support me by giving me the confidence, or whatever, to work through those kinds of things. But I found that sometimes academic women were just like the guys with ties. To be successful in a male academic environment maybe they had to become just as efficient and impersonal as the men, perhaps forgetting what it was like to struggle with finding childcare or having no money.

Petra: I guess I haven't thought about mentoring as a concept or a part of my life or even a role for me until my graduate school experience because I have had so few mentors. Except for...I look back on the women who have influenced me. You know, what women provided role models for me as a young female, or girl? It was my aunt and two teachers, all of whom were single, independently supported themselves and were, to some degree or another, intellectual. Miss Francis, my English teacher, was an ex-nun, dressed like a man, very serious, you know, who worked us so hard in terms of our writing, our reading. It was through her that I read Willa Cather, and got introduced to the first women writers. And then my biology teacher was Miss Jacquat who was the typical spinster teacher—the gray hair, with the bun, the wool suits…tight buttoned up shirts—she was the most rigorous teacher. I worked my butt off for these women. I wanted their approval because they were smart and they were very demanding and they didn't accept mediocre work. Then there was my aunt, who was the one I could talk about politics or current events with. I remember over Thanksgiving holidays and Christmas holidays the family coming over and us talking about Russia and Communism and the Cold War and politics and the presidential elections and that she was the only other person in the family I could do that with—nuclear war…all these topics that were of interest to me. And then Caryn became my friend when I was fourteen or fifteen and we were in French together. She was doing advanced placement Spanish and was reading Spanish literature. I was reading German, Hesse, Goethe, and we talked to each other about a lot of intellectual things. But that's it.

Jan: That is very interesting, I can remember an eighth grade teacher very fondly because she did project work and she did things that were more fun but I think of most of my elementary teachers as uniformly stern because I guess that was the model for them. I didn't have a woman teacher in high school, except for a woman German teacher, until my senior year when we moved to Arizona. I had come from a school of one hundred kids in a very rural area of Wisconsin to Scottsdale High School and I was just bewildered and exhausted the whole time. I can remember one day when it was very hot. I had English with a Mrs. Lowenstein who taught A.P. Literature. She said to me, "Don't do too much, you're not a strong person". I said, "What do you mean?" Rural girls were supposed to be strong—there was pride in that. She said, "No, no, take care of yourself. This may be too much. Let go a little bit." I can remember being so amazed that a teacher could be concerned about me as a person and would make such a kind comment to me. I had had these teachers who were just not involved with students personally, except perhaps to catch them at things. Another difference, I don't remember having women teachers as an undergraduate at the university either. I can't remember a single one. Or in my M.A. program, either, except for a wonderful woman who was adjunct faculty in school psychology. It was not until I came back for my doctorate in 1977 that I remember having women teachers at the university. If you think about it, it's astounding, just astounding. You know, I feel that I've always had to carve stuff out for myself. The delight of working with the women in the research group was that we took care of each other, mentored each other, regardless of our roles.

Petra: I think it's real difficult to sort out all the issues about mentoring because there are so many personal issues. I can't say that I don't have questions about what the basis of our relationship is or about any relationship with a woman, because there has been so much distrust for me in relationships with women. It's not that I don't trust women, but I grew up thinking that women just had relationships with men, that's who we were supposed to trust.

Jan: Again, it is interesting. I think back to not having close women friends from about tenth grade until I was in my thirties and in graduate school…this immensely long period of my life when my closest relationships, all my friendships, were with men, and then I rediscovered the importance of friendships with women and now I'm unraveling my 60's socialization and valuing relationships with both men and women. For a long time, I struggled with that powerful socialization you described and the hard work it took to commit to friendships with women.

Petra: We are raised to see other women as competitors for male interest. There aren't even role models or examples of women's friendships which is why *Thelma and Louise* and *Fried Green Tomatoes* really spoke to me. I think back on some of the literature that I've been reading recently. It's still all about individual women like Kate Chopin in *The Great Awakening* or Jean Rhys' work. It is the woman alone trying to deal with her place and her identity and yes they are grappling with the same issues that I am, but they are doing it in that male way which is an independent…

Jan: In that room looking over the park or whatever ocean beach you are near…

Petra: Right. This very romaticized view of solitude and the individual and making it on their own which on the one hand is very attractive…

Jan: And yet lonely…devastating in its silence.

"Seeing Pieces of Yourself Die": Maintaining Identity

Petra: Well, I find myself—it's like walking on egg shells all the time and trying to balance that. Getting my own students, having my own area of expertise and carving a spot for myself but not wanting to come across as too strong, and I always make sure that I'm advising students to also take other people's classes to acknowledge them and to make sure that they know that I'm not too uppity or look down on their work and respect them. There is no place in academe to build collaborative relationships, to acknowledge that every colleague has something to offer and that I have one area of expertise and a role that I can play on a thesis committee and you form the whole picture by having three or four people on a committee, which makes sense to me. But that's the way it should be and we should be respecting that difference and seeing the strength that it brings rather than this need for one person to control it all.

Jan: About half way through my third year at Oregon I started advising a lot of students on my own and students started switching to me, and suddenly…I was not asked to be on certain dissertation committees the last two years. I saw that as a rejection of me for being too powerful…for attracting some of the students. It was so overt. At first I was on committees that I didn't know anything about and then suddenly there were committees I should have been on because of my expertise and I wasn't asked.

Petra: Yes. Well, it's the issue that I have now, the discomfort that I have with not being too good because then you become a threat and with that a sense of tension and distrust and, you know, I don't want to alienate people. To me it is just so clear that what any of us do as women in academe is going to reflect on all of us, because we are a minority, on the margins, always walking a tightrope. So, there is a pressure that I put on myself and that I assume other women also have, that we have to be careful. We have to present ourselves so we don't reflect badly on each other because if one of us makes a mistake…you know.

Jan: I had a student who was being very resistant. I was in the position as the bad professor who had this student who didn't know how to play by the rules. She tried to make her own rules and I felt I was being criticized for permitting it.

Petra: Yes, I don't want to betray my female grad students. I will not make them the sacrificial lamb for my relationships with other people in the department.

Jan: I think one reason our relationship has continued is that I don't feel responsible for you in anyway. That's not meant to be negative.

Petra: No.

Jan: I don't have to be responsible for you.

Petra: Well, that's what makes it…you know, I think that's why we continue to work together. This is the first time that I took a trip to do specifically work, my work, on a variety of levels. But to me the fact is that we did get together and decided we needed a weekend for just the two of us, you know, to do some work together and spend some time together. Because that's going to be the way that we maintain this relationship.

Jan: By also going to bookstores and goofing around a bit.

Petra: Well, I think part of my commitment to meeting with you, you know, or doing things like this, is to disrupt business as usual and nine to five. My fear too, of somehow getting co-opted in the suburban lifestyle of nine to five. That just scares me to death. I will do a lot to disrupt that…and not lead a normal life.

Jan: And see pieces of yourself die. I mean all those months in Michigan when the last thing I wanted to do was leave my house. I thought, this is really scary. I see what happens to people. It's so snug. You can really be tempted to give up on yourself.

Anything You Want—Anything At All

Jan: I know this whole thing was my fault. I know it.

Petra: Damn it, there's one thing you should know by now—this wasn't your fault.

Jan: No matter what happens, I'm glad you came along with me.

Petra: Hold on.

Jan: I guess everything from here on in could be pretty awful.

Petra: Unbearable, I'd imagine.

Jan: You're a good friend.

Petra: You too, sweetie, the best. How do you like the trip so far.

Jan: I guess we went a little crazy, huh?

Petra: No, we've always been crazy. This is just the first chance we've had to really express ourselves.

Jan: So, what the hell is this, anyway?

Petra: Well I don't know. It's awesome enough to be the goddamn Grand Canyon.

Jan: Yeah—isn't it beautiful.

Petra: It's something else, allright.

You Got It

Jan: Oh, my god, it looks like the thought police.

Petra: All this just for us?

Amorphous Voice: Place your hands in plain view. Any failure to obey this command will be considered an act of aggression.

Jan: What are you doing?

Petra: I'm not giving up.

The Voice: I repeat. Cut your dialogue and place your ideas in plain view.

Jan: OK then, let's don't get caught.

Petra: What are you talking about?

Jan: Let's keep going.

Petra: What do you mean?

Jan: Go!

Petra: You sure?

Jan: You got it.

References

Cizek, G. (1995). Crunchy granola and the hegemony of the narrative. *Educational Reseacher, 24*, 26-28.

Hirsch, M. (1989). *The mother/daughter plot: Narrative, psychoanalysis, feminism.* Bloomington: Indiana University Press.

Jipson, J., Munro, P., Victor, S., Jones, K., & Freed-Rowland, G. (1995). *Repositioning feminism and education: Perspectives on educating for social change.* Westport, CT: Bergin & Garvey.

CHAPTER ELEVEN

JANICE JIPSON
NICHOLAS PALEY

Method: Who Am I?

When We Work Now

4:28 p.m. PST
May 5, 1995

Method: Who Am I?

When We Work Now

4:28 p.m. PST
May 5, 1995

When we work now, we don't know where we're going to end up. We start with something, and end up with something very different. We begin with an idea that interests us, but very quickly it becomes many ideas. It splits apart into pieces. We split apart into pieces. Our one idea becomes a kind of jumble. It explodes into something like a monkey puzzle, a cactus. We become a cactus to ourselves. If we look carefully, we can sometimes recognize our competing assurances about research, our various political and conceptual motivations, our different senses of self, and our fears which we want and don't want to say. So there's an idea which almost immediately becomes an impossibility. A tangle of internal logic. Systems of competing voice. Inner and Outer space. And then long moments of silence when we wonder: How to put things together now?

We work in fits and starts. No line. No ending. No thought anymore of proof, of validity, of explanation. Of being good. Separated by geography, economics, family and work schedules, personal history, and even the shape of our own strange dreams, we feel that we are nevertheless connected. Sometimes we think that we admire our friendship more than our act of writing itself. Our work does not start with theory, but always with something else. Is it love?

When we work now, we are all over the place. Logic is an inferno that feeds us in the roar of its mind. Edging down the path, feeling its blaze on our eyes and faces, we move on. There's a map that someone gave us once. Where did we leave it? The phone rings and rings and rings in obvious places, but we've tried to train ourselves to listen for other things. Rings of what?

When we work now, there are bills to
pay; still we are intrigued by the functions of chance and the unconscious.
Where did we first read about that and
forget? Love letters we've saved remind
us of their powerful radiance. Or certain
(parts of) poems. Long ago, one of us
remembers (it was in high school), reading Rilke and how that head-on collision
bashed at the doors of our heart. When
did we forget its all-out war for our
whole spirit? For the existence of impossibilities?

When we work now, we try to find colorings in our writings that we abandoned so long ago (in the lives we abandoned so long ago?). Finish is no longer anything. Stopping and starting get confused. Direction? We did that. Leave everything rough and uneven now so you can see the spaces in between where things don't connect and don't force them. Where your mind struggles to translate what it sees anyway. Could that be a practice? Stumbling, along the way, or crawling, we work with whatever occupies us. It can be anything and everything. Take what you find on your way (or in your way), and put it there too.

When we work now, similarities never compete. We scrounge. We descend. We get turned around and when we put something down, we wonder: OK, this something next to that something next to that something. What do we see? What is that image telling us? We try to fill our little beach pails with all the sea and sand we could never quite get in them so many summers ago. Sometimes it's so easy now, and sometimes it's hard. Sand and sea. Scrounging and sleep. Scrounging for a rose that grows out of the rock. Or is it the other way round? Scrounging for a way on our way. All you have to do is choose. When we work now.

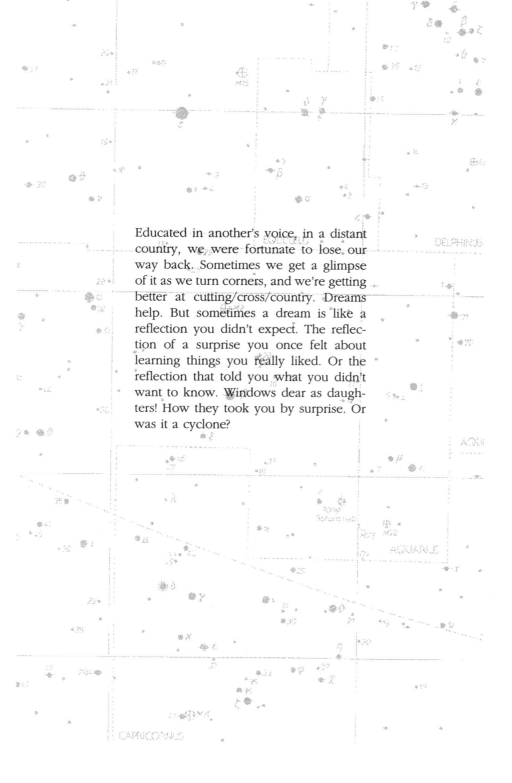

Educated in another's voice, in a distant
country, we were fortunate to lose our
way back. Sometimes we get a glimpse
of it as we turn corners, and we're getting
better at cutting/cross/country. Dreams
help. But sometimes a dream is like a
reflection you didn't expect. The reflection of a surprise you once felt about
learning things you really liked. Or the
reflection that told you what you didn't
want to know. Windows dear as daughters! How they took you by surprise. Or
was it a cyclone?

When we work now, we often remember what we were then. When we were in love for the second or third time and not in any precise way when anyone you knew could say that this experience was the direct result of some dependent or independent variable, or an outcome, or a prediction for future research.... We remember how one Saturday afternoon (it was in late March and when by complete chance) we stopped into a gallery off Russell Square to get out of the rain and we saw for the first time some of the impossible assemblies of discarded things by Kurt Schwitters. How long had we been lost from them? We were blown away by the roughness of their thrown away power and by the delicateness of their thrown away power and by the roughness of our loneliness and the impossibilities of that spring before we came to work now.

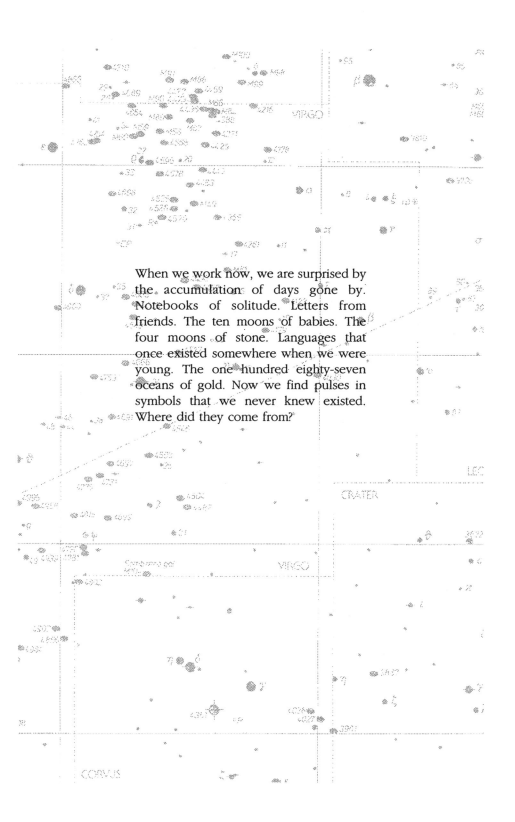

When we work now, we are surprised by
the accumulation of days gone by.
Notebooks of solitude. Letters from
friends. The ten moons of babies. The
four moons of stone. Languages that
once existed somewhere when we were
young. The one hundred eighty-seven
oceans of gold. Now we find pulses in
symbols that we never knew existed.
Where did they come from?

When we work now, no top, no bottom.
No back, no front. No under, no over, no
symmetry. No yard we own. Heap ideas
on top of ideas until they give us their
own shape anywhere. Sometimes this
can be startling—sometimes a mess.
Sometimes this results in a hunger for
something we can't name. The idea of
heaps obsesses us. Their ridiculous
shape. Refusing organization. Refusing to
be a building. Refusing their destiny to
be an architecture. Their density is what
really attracts us. We often wonder now:
What else possibly could?

When we work now, we're tired of little
sentences and big sentences and para-
graphs and conclusions. We like pretexts.
(Pre-texts?) We're surprised by beauty's
renewal in these kinds of forms when
there's still no official name for it. Or
norm. We're surprised about how their
small cyclones blow us away when we
work now. We still get surprised at how
easily we can still be eaten alive and how
that relates to everything else in its own
undefined ways.

When we work now, what else is there?
We're tumbling. Deep snow? A deadline
to meet? An endless column that reminds
us of the endless way to go? Is there a
lesson to learn or teach? Can you really
hear the words? The format? The whole
production? (Through our numbness, can
we ever really hear the words??)

When we work now, everything changes
without letting us know. It gets harder
and harder to hear. It gets harder and
harder to stop. It gets harder and harder
to know.

When we work now, we can often feel
our hands navigating like faces: No
shorelines.

(This is commitment too.)

Santa Rosa, California